THE JOURNEY CONTINUES

THE BIRTH OF A PSALMIST/PROPHET

WILLIAM HATFIELD

ACKNOWLEDGEMENTS

We are all on a journey through life! I want to thank all my family and friends who stand besides me and encourage me when times are tough.

I especially want to thank my aunt Viola for all her advice in editing and preparing the manuscript for publishing.

TABLE OF CONTENTS

Acknowledgment..................................2
Dedication......................................4
Prologue..5
Psalmist..7
The call.......................................74
Confirmation of the call.......................89
The anointing.................................128
Evidence of the anointing.....................135
Dreams..146
Visions.......................................178
Encouragement.................................202
Bio...203

DEDICATION

I dedicate this book to the thirsty and hungry saints of god that desire an intimacy with the Holy Spirit like no other. My prayer is that you can find this journey as a source of encouragement, strength and power to overcome life's struggles and walk in a greater sense of freedom and relationship with the Holy Spirit and all within your sphere of influence.

PROLOGUE

This book is about the journey of a young man called into the five-fold ministry. Being introduced to Jesus as a 6 year old was exciting, but growing in your relationship with god is not what I thought it might be.

My love for god was never in question as I began to grow in hearing the multitude ways that he communicates with his creation. Dreams; visions; and prophetic words of encouragement; through other people. This is the journey of a young man discovering relationship with the Holy Spirit verses religion of church. We are all on a journey that will continue on into eternity.

Everybody's journey is different so let's have grace and love for each other and except that god never created cookie cutter Christians. By sharing our individual journeys with each other we can come into the revelation knowledge of the goodness of god in our lives.

PSALMIST

A psalmist of today would be one whose heart is after the heart of God. He would be one who delights to be in the presence of God and even longs to be. It would be his chief joy. He would be one who finds the time and the place to be alone with Him and has an intimate relationship with Him. He would find the time just to be quiet and still with Him and even basks in His presence. He is like a painter with a blank canvas. The atmosphere is his canvas. He paints the mood in which the Holy Spirit is to move among His people. Sometimes his canvas takes on the mood of healing, sometimes gladness, and sadness, laughing in the spirit or whatever the need is.

The psalmist has to be sensitive to what the Spirit is leading him to and flow in accordance. There is much mature fruit of the Spirit displayed in his life and also the gifts of the Holy Spirit. The Word of the Lord flows freely through him.

The psalms I would like to share are a reflection of God's heart to His people; A reflection of God's people to their creator. The psalms are a reflection of God's people to each other. I began writing psalms in 1988-1989 to the present. The first one was while I was attending my first year bible college. I was severely bored with the first year; it was like Sunday school classes when you were a preteen and you are twenty now. I was meditating on the Lord when I heard these words in my spirit.

RESURRECTION DAY

Once upon a time, long, long ago
My Spirit broke forth to show
The mighty power of the Lord

To bring judgment like a sword

From this time I have gone
To bring forth grace with a song
This very day you shall see
Glorious power with victory

When my power starts to flood
Honor my presence through the blood
When I come this very night
Resurrection power giving sight

Glorious power you shall see
Coming forth to victory
To my church I shall say
You have entered a special day

Be bold, strong and diligent
My resurrection power I have sent
To my church I shall say
Get ready! It's Resurrection Day!!

I wrote the words down quite calmly and after I read them I was excited. Something inside of me said the Holy Spirit has given me a new gift. Not sure what it was but I noticed the poem rhymed and it was prophetic in nature. I was later to learn this was the definition of a psalm. I showed my classmates and they were as intrigued as I. Later that day during another class something else started happening. I would glance at a classmate and an intense curiosity would rise up in me regarding them. I would hear words in my spirit and write them down. To my surprise they would ask how I knew the spiritual meaning to their name. I didn't I was just writing what I heard in my spirit. The students became excited and asked me to write a psalm for them. I just prayed because I knew I wasn't in charge but it was a prophetic gift of the Holy Spirit and it would only manifest as He wills. Over the years until 2017 I have wrote a few hundred psalms for people. I am sharing this psalm of an individual with her permission.

LAURIE

To the daughter of faith
Saved by the power of grace
Resurrection strength strong and true
Comes upon my daughter to do

Victories are coming so rejoice
Blessings are abundant, make your choice
Boldness and confidence to you belong
Resurrection power in a song

Boldly proclaim my resurrected word
Signs and wonders for those who heard
My glory shall be revealed
My word to you is a shield

Be strong and excited, filled with love
On you is my spirit from above
Go forth in victory do not fear

Resurrection power to those who hear

    I found this gift exciting as it took in many aspects of life. I found myself writing so regularly that I thought it was an endless supply. I want to jump ahead a few years to a time when the church I attended operated a booth called angels tent. This booth was at a county festival the town was having. The purpose of the booth was in response to a physic tent that read your palms and told your future according to Satan's will. The pastor brought in a facilitator who knew how to train people to move in the prophetic. You may say O' Come on. Let me tell you it is easier than you think.

Acts 2:17-21

King James Version

17 And it shall come to pass in the last days, said God, I will pour out of my Spirit upon all flesh: and your sons and your daughters shall prophesy, and your young men shall see visions, and your old men shall dream dreams:
18 And on my servants and on my handmaidens I will pour out in those days of my Spirit; and they shall prophesy:
19 And I will shew wonders in heaven above, and signs in the earth beneath; blood, and fire, and vapor of smoke:
20 The sun shall be turned into darkness, and the moon into blood, before that great and notable day of the Lord come:

21 And it shall come to pass, that whosoever shall call on the name of the Lord shall be saved.

    The whole body of Christ has the ability to prophesy and move in the manifestations of the Holy Spirit. It's just unbelief that stops people from doing the works of God. People would come in and sit at one of the six tables we had in operation and receive a word from the Lord. If the facilitator at the table wasn't getting anything from the Holy Spirit they were trained to fall back on a scripture, Jeremiah 29:11
for I know the plans I have for you," says the LORD. "They are plans for good and not for disaster, to give you a future and a hope.

I would write poems for people and they would go away excited and happy that the God of heaven would take time to communicate with them. Religion has taught us that the God of heaven is not interested in communicating with us. However the opposite is true. God desires fellowship with His people.
2 Corinthians 13:14. May the grace of the Lord Jesus Christ, and the love of God, and the fellowship of the Holy Spirit be with you all.

Over a two day period we had one-hundred and fifty new decisions for Jesus and seventy-five recommitments. I took a break and went for a walk and noticed the Spirit of God dealing with individuals in the crowd. When I got back to the angel tent the Spirit of God instructed me to go in the back to the intercession prayer area and pray. As I prayed the Spirit of the Lord gave me four poems with the instructions to give them the facilitators at the table. If the facilitator got nothing then they were to give the Individual a poem. One poem was about the Spirit of God sitting down with a musician and writing songs together. You guessed it; an individual who was a musician sat down and got that poem. He went away quite excited.

Another poem was about having a second chance. Earlier a couple of sisters sat at a table and received a word from the Lord and one of them accepted Jesus. The other said no. it was getting on into the evening so the one sister decided it was time to go home and cook dinner for her family. The other sister decided to come back to the angel tent and see if maybe God had something privately for her. The facilitator at her table was getting nothing, and then she remembered the poem. She handed the woman the poem explaining how someone in the back who never seen her wrote it specifically for her. The woman read it then broke down and cried telling her story. She was here earlier but decided not to accept Jesus. The poem spoke directly to that situation encouraging her of God's great love for her. She accepted Jesus and went away a new creation.

Back to the bible college; where this gift was in its infancy and being enjoyed by all. After a few days of writing for people I got a poem dealing with wives.

A GODLY WIFE

Virtuous and compassionate full of love
She is God's gift sent from above
To this woman I shall impart
Wisdom and knowledge to fill her heart

The fear of the Lord makes her just
In her, her husband does trust
To this woman I shall say
Receive my anointing this very day

I shall guide you through your life
Receive my anointing dear Godly wife
Integrity and honor are yours to stay
You shall be blessed day by day.

I read this poem to the class and right away they wanted one about a Godly husband. I told them I would pray about it and I did and within an hour I received this poem.

A GODLY HUSBAND

Prophet, Priest and a King
The Word of God he does bring
Protects and serves from a pure heart
Being a provider is but a start

He is the image and glory of the Lord
Fearlessly wielding the two edged sword
A strong, bold and powerful life
He'll gladly lay it down for his wife

Love and compassion from who does flow
To him his wife will gladly go
A strong bridge over the pressures of life

He'll be blessed with a godly wife.

    I was surprised when one woman said that wasn't quite what she was looking for. I told her to go to God and get one for herself. I just write what I hear in my spirt and it isn't up to me if people like them or not. As time continued I would get inspiration from many different sources. I knew I was writing about a person when the curiosity factor rose. Most of the psalms I write seem to flow in a rhyming factor but I soon found out that this would not be a pattern set in stone. Here is an example.

DEAN

I see a hot air balloon flying high above the clouds. Dean and VI are in the basket. Ropes are hanging from the basket. People are reaching for and grabbing the ropes. When they grasp the ropes, the ropes along with the people must be transported higher than the balloon, thus making the hot air balloon a launching off place. As hot air sends a natural balloon higher so shall the wind of my spirit launch and carry your balloon higher and guide its direction to places and heights only dreamed of. Are you ready to lift others higher than what you perceive you are?

Bible College was a unique experience where the anointing of a psalmist began but never gave me a direction for my life. It just left me with a large student loan to pay back. I am not against Bible College and if you sense the Holy Spirit telling you to go then you should have gone already. I went because of pressure from pastors and other spiritual leaders. Funny thing was they never mentioned that I might think about the school across the river. I was to attend their school which was a part of their church. Enough rambling, after completing the two year course I left and found the psalmist anointing increased. There is only so much you can do in the four walls of the church or religious setting. The real ministry starts where people live their lives every day not just three hours a week. I wish I could find the song from the eighties that was my favorite. Some of the lyrics were, "some people want a position within the churches four walls but I want a ministry a yard from the gates of hell." If someone reading this knows the song and how I can get it please let me know. I am on Facebook like most of the North American population.

I love this anointing because there is no rhyme or reason on how it kicks in. I am driving down the highway and my attention was drawn to a tree sitting in the middle of a field by itself. This is the psalm that came from that situation.

HOME

Alone and majestic it does stand
Strong arms reaching out so grand
Bringing protection to those below
An umbrella from the deep snow

Standing upright in an open field

To others its fruit to yield
What is this sight I see?
But a lonely spruce tree

Many look and see no good
Just a big old chunk of wood
But to the animals which do roam
This tree is called home

There is a moral to this psalm
Don't condemn just be calm
Others may not measure up
But who's to say what's their cup

This psalm so reminded me of a church I attended. During the eighties my first wife and I had a ministry among street people. We won bikers, prostitutes and witches to Jesus. We would bring them to church hoping to incorporate them into the fold. Problem was they didn't look like the rest of the suits and ties and were looked down on. Realizing this we started a bible study with them and it began to grow. We were sitting with over thirty with children when it caught the attention of the church leaders. I attended this church on a regular basis because I was part of its bible college. I was called in and told that I couldn't have a bible study. I explained the situation about bringing them but they were being looked down by other members of the congregation. As soon as I told them that these street people were gladly donating large sums of money to the church the attitude changed. I was told I could have a bible study but the people could only come for a month then I would have to send them away. I could not do that because it takes more than a month to make newly born again sinners into saints. Discipleship takes time and you can't force it. Nevertheless I had a choice to make, the religious institution or people. I chose people and left the church. Some of the people wanted us to start a church but sad to say that adventure wasn't in the cards. I was really disappointed when friends of mine who still attended the church told me the pastor was preaching against me. He was telling the congregation not to attend any bible study or meeting I might have because I had a demonic influence over people.

How are we going to win the lost to Jesus with this sort of pettiness in the church? Be careful on how you judge.

Matthew 7:1-3King James Version (KJV)

7 Judge not, that ye be not judged.

2 For with what judgment ye judge, ye shall be judged: and with what measure ye mete, it shall be measured to you again.

³ And why beholdest thou the mote that is in thy brother's eye, but considerest not the beam that is in thine own eye?

We eventually found places for the people to fellowship in before we left Saskatoon. I heard a few years later that some of the natives that attended our study started their own church. It wasn't long after the pastor preached against me that some of the under handed activities of the leadership came to light. Money raised for projects seemed to vanish and the pastor built himself a new house in a gated community and a cabin by the lake. The church is but a shell of what it used to be. I am not saying that stuff happened because of the pastor coming against me. I am saying if God is moving in a direction you are not familiar with please don't make judgments because they will come back to bite you. I believe we are living in Revelation 2-3 where God is judging the church to prepare it for the resurrection. God desires us to be humble and not judge by what we see in the natural.

Done Bible College with this great word of encouragement from the dean, "don't be discouraged if you don't get into any kind of ministry you dreamed about because eighty percent of bible college graduates never enter into ministry." Thanks a lot why did you pressure me to attend your college for two years if there is no ministry future for me afterwards. Oh well I guess that was the course of life. So you go find a job and continue to support your family but now a large student loan to pay off as well.

So you do what every person does. You talk with God about it and rest knowing god has everything in control. I heard many sermons on waiting on the Lord. Problem was I am not the waiting type, if I think it I try to do it immediately. The Lord gave me some encouragement with the following psalms.

WAIT UPON THE LORD

Those who wait upon the Lord
Shall be tempered as a two edged sword
They shall walk and not tire
The anointing of God lifts them higher

They shall run and not pass out
In victory songs they do shout
Honor and integrity are their lot
The grace of God they have sought

They shall mount up with wings as an eagle
Splendorous they soar, O so regal
They shall walk in robes of royal thread
Blessed be the Word I have read.

I guess just trust the Lord and put my hand to the plow and don't look back. One thing I did know after experiencing the ministry team and pastor of that church organization I was turned off on being a pastor, I even commented on that to the head pastor. I guess being a young Christian with no diplomacy developed in my life I never knew not to burn bridges, I just blew them up. I guess you would expect that from a carnal Christian with more zeal than wisdom.

The thing I rejoiced in was that God knew my heart even if my head was in la la land. My heart was after God and I just needed to grow more in the spirit. The Lord gave me the following psalm to encourage me.

A SPIRITUAL MAN

A spiritual man upright and true
Integrity and love thru and thru
Spiritual pride is not his lot
The grace of God he has sought

A spiritual man quite contagious
Against him the enemy rages
Victories are known through the land
In the power of God he must stand

A spiritual man faithful and true
With him no days are blue
A priest and king he shall be
When Jesus comes for you and me.

After Bible College everything seemed to fall apart. No job and Christmas was around the corner so you do what you know to do and that is talk with God. Not like most prayer meetings I have experienced where people have a list of request that they talk at God about but never wat around to hear His response. The Lord gave me this psalm to encourage me.

FAITHFULNESS

I will exalt my only hope
Through your Word I can cope
When life is futile, full of disaster
I shall jump, shout, be filled with laughter

When my world comes crashing down
I'll sing and dance with no frown
Because of kindness, grace, and love
I shall praise you who is above

A new day is dawning I shall see
Your Word will guide through eternity
In song and dance I have praised
On that third day you were raised

Praise and thanks I stand strong
Because to whom I do belong
You are my hope, mighty king
I will praise you in everything.

Christmas was coming and we were invited to go to Grande Prairie and spend it with my cousin. We got in our little chevette and headed down the highway, only to have the engine blow in minus forty weather. I pulled over to the side of the road put on my four way flashers, lifted the hood of my car and the steam and oil poured out. Thank God he knew ahead of time my situation and had a trucker a couple of miles behind me. This sixteen wheeler semi pulled over and we loaded our luggage into his rig along with my wife and our two small children. He drove us to Edmonton where we met up with my sister and borrowed their little truck to go the rest of the way to Grande Prairie for Christmas vacation. I rejoiced because our helper the Holy Spirit saved us from a potential life threatening situation.

FEAR NOT

Fear not, fear not, and fear not
I am the salvation you have sought
To deliver you by the power of my blood
The enemy may roar but he's no flood

Through the power of my name
To you salvation has already came
Fear not, fear not, and fear not!
My blood your salvation has bought

Fear not! Look to the king on high
Let your praises ascend to the sky
Resurrection power on the way
To deliver from harm every day.

HELPER

The helper is one to whom you must run
When battles are to be won
Imparting bravery, strength and might
Be valiant, be brave, and continue to fight

When in weakness, lost or confused
Resist the enemy, don't be abused
The helper is there to lend a hand
In the power of God you shall stand

Who is this helper? What's His name?
The Holy Spirit, the one and the same
The enemy comes, bringing strife
Run to the author of all life

He is your help in time of need
Of His instruction do take heed
Author of life to one and all
Bless God! I'm redeemed from the fall.

Christmas came and went and with the help of my sister and brother in law we moved to Edmonton Alberta to start a new life. I was glad that God brought people into our lives to encourage us because life was looking pretty bleak at this time.

THE ENCOURAGER

Who is this one who brings encouragement?
Obviously one whom heaven has sent
She reaches out when others are down
Imparting hope and smiles
In the place of a frown

Who is this one from whom strength flows
On her my anointing continually grows
Bringing joy and peace to all her peers
She reaches out to wipe their tears

To this child I shall say,
My peace on you shall continually stay
To the one who looks to others best?
Enter thou into my Holy rest.

I took a job as a maintenance man at an apartment complex. After about six months I moved back to Grande Prairie where I am living today. Ordained in 1998 and served as an associate pastor for a few years. I did the work of the ministry that was set before me. I resumed my job as a roofer to provide for my family. Ministry seemed lost and going nowhere so I just relaxed and worked as a roofer. The psalms started coming randomly with no pattern at all. The subjects varied. One particular day when life seemed discouraging and the wife was looking at you like you were just a dreamer and nothing of reality would be produced in your life; the Lord gave me this psalm.

HUSBAND TO HIS WIFE

To the one who's a gift from above
You are beautiful in whom I find love
Please be patient with me every day
I sometimes get confused and lose my way

Don't be angry or full of strife
I too am filled with resurrection life
Please be an encourager when my days are blue
Because truly, I do love you

I am being changed; God's tugging at my heart
Life's a challenge; I want to do my part
Hold me tight, I need your love
Cut me slack, don't push or shove

I am a man who's sensitive at heart
But my feelings I don't easily impart
Soon I will rise up in the right hour

Flowing with God's resurrection power.

When you are doing a job that becomes routine and you can think you can do it in your sleep; you pray in the spirit while you work. This is some of the fruit of praying in tongues while you worked. I had to keep a notepad and pen handy because I never knew when I was going to get a psalm. I remembered a dream I had when I was just a few months old as a Christian and this psalm explains it exactly.

THE BLOOD

Standing on the edge of the universe
Proclaiming the Word, but not in verse
Standing tall and strong
Proclaiming words that weren't wrong

Bold and confident I have said
His precious blood has been shed
There I stand where all could see
Proclaiming the blood for eternity

Of His blood I do not plead
Boldness and confidence is what I read
Proclamation of that great name
The powerful blood I will PROCLAIM!!!!

One Sunday I was asked to preach. I brought the children up for prayer and prayed and dismiss them to their classes. Watching the children put the seed for a psalm in my heart.

CHILDREN

Wide eyed and innocent of all wrong
Sit the children of this psalm
Confident, trusting, willing to share
The love they experience there

Through these doors my children come
To learn the integrity of my Son
The teachers have quite the task
To answer questions the pupils ask

Love, kindness and righteousness they yearn
Please help my children to learn

Teachers walk upright, do your part
To give the children a righteous start.

After church services you usually go for lunch with friends. Every now and then you end up with a large group of people. The following psalm was written at the table while the group was eating and fellowshipping.

COMPANIONS

When we are among friends
The anointing He does send
To keep our thoughts on high
For our praises to ascend to the sky

We are a cheerful joyous lot
The grace of God we have sought
Let us encourage and strengthen each other
There's a friend who sticks closer than a brother

Red, white, yellow and blue
Will we be friends quite true?

Looking to the others best
Let's pursue the Word with zest.

As I began to grow in the anointing of a psalmist I found myself writing psalms for people who were going through negative situations in life. People need love expressed from God to them continually because this world pulls them down. This psalm I wrote to one of God's daughters. No name was mentioned so it can be piggy backed by every daughter of God who needs encouragement.

DAUGHTER OF THE LORD

To this young child I shall say
Rejoice, rejoice, coming is a better day
Strength and honor I shall impart
To my daughter of a gentle heart

My love extends with resurrection life
Walk in love not in strife
To my daughter I shall say
Search my heart, continue to pray

To the daughter of my grace
I behold your lovely face
I rejoice because your mine
To you my love will forever shine.

Sorry if it seems like I am bouncing from subject to subject but that is how the psalms started coming. No rhyme or reason just random. This next psalm came because of the end times we are living in and Satan is raging in fury across the planet.

DEVIL'S DEMISE

The anointing is flowing
The gifts are growing
The devil is in fear
Because his end is near
When the devil roars in strife
Know for sure he's at the end of his life
Though he connives and does try
Know for sure his attempts will die
Victory is yours for sure
Because of a heart that's pure

Jesus Christ the King on high
Has destroyed the enemy, it's time for him to die

We are in a spiritual war and when you walk in holiness you can say what Jesus said in john 14:30 New International Version I will not say much more to you, for the prince of this world is coming. He has no hold over me. It is easier to do warfare when we are walking upright before god then the devil can't bring railing accusations against us and we have victory over his attacks. We go through battles and experience victories again and again. It seems to be endless and we just want to give up but we know there is one to who we can look.

GOD OF COMFORT

My Savior and hope of whom I'll sing
Guides and comforts in everything
To my soul he does impart
His mighty peace to settle my heart

When the entire world roars with strife

His great love brings me life
From the cross come blessings more
The chastisement for our peace He has bore

When confusion turns my head
Of His Word I have read
Quiet and confidence is my part
Peace and comfort does fill my heart.

Our focus has to be on Jesus because He is the only one that can give us a life worth living.

GOD IN THE HIGHEST

Praise be to God from whom all blessings flow
With love and worship, to Him I shall go
He is my fortress and strong tower
My Jesus comes with resurrection power

He is the light and joy of life
Keeping me from harm and all strife
He is my soon coming King
Bringing joy and causing all to sing

He is the one who looks to my best
Giving joy, peace and eternal rest
Of all the things that come my way
I'll look forward to resurrection day.

When others demean you and act like you have no value remember there is someone who values you beyond measure.

GOD'S BEST

You are worth more than you know
Study my Word, continue to grow
Be strong, you're a child of the king
Success and honor in everything

Your destiny brings ultimate success

Don't say no, just say yes
Full of life you shall be
When in faith you look to me

Excitement and power, the fruit of life
Wisdom and honor, the absence of strife
Grace and wonders, child of the King
You are blessed in everything.
No matter what a person goes
through we have an anchor.

THE WORD

The Word is precious to me
Upholding and strengthening for eternity
The Word brings healing this I know
In times of trouble to the Word I go

Powerful, living, sharp and quick
The Word delivers those that are sick
In the Word I find sustenance
Guiding and directing to repentance

I'm in love with the righteous Word
Inspiring faith in all who heard

The Father, the Word, the Holy One
Set free to worship the righteous Son.

With all the activity in my life one thing stands out. The desire I had when I talked with Jesus when I was ten. To be a preacher, not necessarily a pastor but a preacher.

PREACHER

To be a preacher of the Word
Blessing the many who have heard
To skillfully wield the two edged sword
Being a vessel of the Lord

Son of man hear my Word
Bless the many who have heard
Store my sayings in your heart
Deliver My Word that's your part

Son of man, this I say
Study the Word every day
Go to the people, tell them so
Whether they say yes, whether they say no

Blessed is the Lord from His place
Being a preacher is only through grace
I'll skillfully preach the mighty Word
Blessing the many who have heard.

The more I study God's word the more I realize I need a deeper revelation of God's grace.

GRACE

Amazing grace how sweet the sounds
Because of love that knows no bounds
I was lost in sin and undone
Redeemed through the cross of your only Son

Grace came with blessings by the score
Jesus stands knocking at our heart's door
Will I let the righteous one in?
To save and redeem from the power of sin

Hosanna in the highest, Holy, Holy one

I receive you in my heart, Jesus the Son
Because of grace you were raised
Forever now to be praised.
 As my journey in life continues I find one place I desire to be above all else and that is in His presence.

THE PRESENCE

With pureness of heart I shall stand
In your presence O so grand
Majestic angels all around
Rejoicing! A glorious sound

I shall stand before you on that day
Until then I will continue to pray
Your presence, I have sought
With your blood I was bought

I am a child of the most high
In your presence, my tears you shall dry
In your presence I shall stand
Rejoicing in song O so grand.
I found the fastest way into the presence of God is to honor the blood of Christ.

THE BLOOD

Standing on the edge of the universe
Proclaiming the Word, but not in verse
Standing tall and strong
Proclaiming words that weren't wrong

Bold and confident I have said
His precious blood has been shed
There I stand where all could see
Proclaiming the blood for eternity

Of His blood I do not plead
Boldness and confidence is what I read
Proclamation of that great name
The powerful blood I will PROCLAIM!!!!

Earlier I mentioned the angel's tent. One thing I forgot to mention was the reason I left the tent and went for a walk. I started to experience an open heaven. When the heavens are open revelation flows so freely it almost is too much h for the soul to handle.

OPEN HEAVENS

Open heavens are the things you want
Closed heavens are the devil's taunts
When you release those rivers of water
The devil shall flee because of his slaughter

When in intercessory prayer you fight
Beams and shafts of Holy light
Shall penetrate the blanket of dark
Be fervent because there is a great spark

Be strong, faithful and ready to fight
Because you shall see darkness blasted by light
Faith and confident you shall stand
Glorious victory o so grand!

When you are operating under an open heaven winning souls to Jesus becomes much easier.

SOULWINNER

Wise, wise, wise is this man you see
Helping others to change their destiny
He is the one who heeds my instruction
Saving others from their own destruction

His love for life you shall know
When reaching to others the anointing flows
To this one full of life
Integrity and honor with no strife

This is a man who knows my ways
Spending time with me, ordering his days
This is a child of the most high
Reaching out until the day he dies.
To be affective at winning people to Jesus you first have to be an effective prayer warrior.

WARRIOR

A warrior is one who stands to fight
For everything he believes is right
Sin and unrighteousness he will not condone
He will continue to stand, even if alone

The weapons of his warfare he does know
The battle cry has sounded; he is the first to go
Wise and cunning he proceeds to fight
For everything he believes to be right

This one is special don't you see
Helping others to attain liberty
Humble and honorable, quite so real
Resurrection power when he kneels

When a battle rages here or there
He shall proceed through Word and prayer

The Lord is raising an army you see
To March to war; on their knees.

I am glad that Jesus chose me to be a psalmist because the revelation I get and the spiritual growth I develop causes joy in my heart. Sometimes I get a picture from God's point of view like the following psalm declares.

MESSIAH

My God! My God! Why do you forsake me?
Great is the suffering, don't you see?
I am the one who paid for sin
Lift your head, stand and grin

I paid the price for all you've done
You are delivered from the evil one
I was raised by great power
It will soon be resurrection hour

Your righteousness is of me
My blood has set you free
I am the Messiah who suffered for you

Accept my love, for it is true

I am exalted, lifted on high
Rejoice, rejoice, and do not cry
I am the Lord who set you free
Forever mine, you shall be.

The messiah has a name and his name is JESUS.

JESUS

Jesus Christ, the Lord my rock
In His presence I shall walk
Glory and strength, full of love
My dear Jesus, sent from above

Strength and honor He will impart
To everyone who is pure of heart
Kindness radiates from His eyes
A man of integrity, with no lies

The Lord my Savior, full of grace
Gentleness shines from His face
Love extends and knows no bound
A greater God, who has found?

It took me awhile but eventually I got the revelation that Jesus paid for our sickness the same time and place, the cross, that he paid for sin.

HEALING

I was bruised for your iniquities
Look to me not your remedies
I am the Lord of all your health
Healing breaks forth in overflowing wealth

I am the healer, great is my supply
Look to me, you shall not die
I was wounded for your transgressions
Your healing comes in many successions

By my stripes you have been healed
With my Spirit you were sealed
Use my name, be so quick
I've delivered you, don't be sick.
The bible says Jesus name is above every name.

THE NAME

The name which is above every name
Power and might found in the same
Love and compassion from who does flow
This precious name we must know

At the sound of the name from above
Every knee shall bow, reaching for love
Of His Lordship they shall confess
Love of that name saints do express

To the exalted name from above
A heart of compassion filled with love
Who is this majestic mighty one?
Jesus Christ, the omnipotent Holy Son.

His name is so high even nature worships Him.

NATURE
The birds, flowers and trees do sing

Rejoicing in the Lord their melodies ring
Watching the sun about half past five
When all of a sudden the breeze was alive

As the breeze continued on bye
The name of Jesus was exalted on high
As the anointing began to flow
A new revelation for me to know

Then one day while reading the Word
All excited over the phrase I heard
Sun, moon and stars of light
Praise His name this very night.

Many Christians fall short of the life Christ has for us. We were never meant to live on barely get by avenue and the corner of lacking street. We were made in the image of God and should be living as overcomers.

VICTORY

The Lord my King, the heavenly rock
Of your exploits I shall talk

You are the one who set me free
Anointed my life for total victory

You have made me more than a conqueror
I'm not beaten, trodden under, or sore
Your divine power has given to us all
Redemption and victory from the fall

When terror comes by night
I'll stand in confidence not in fright
Pestilence comes, I'll not fear
Rejoice in the Word that I hear

You are the one who set me free
Anointed my life for total victory
Living stones to me you talk
I'm a chip off the heavenly rock.

Not only is Jesus my messiah and savior He is also my shepherd who guides me and watches over me.

THE SHEPHERD

O my King! To you I'll sing
You have blessed in everything

All around, the shadow of death
I'm delivered by your breath

The breath of life fills my heart
On the paths of righteousness I shall start
Of the evil I will not fear
Because of your presence O so near

Power and authority I do know
My enemy runs, watch him go
Boldness and mercy all of my life
Quiet times with no strife

I'll live in the house of the Lord
Protected by your two edged sword
Your testimony and covenant I shall keep
Because your anointing guides my feet.

Prosperity and healing preachers are declared as the other gospel which is apparently not of God. I think these people should think twice about judging the Word of God. I think God gives clues to His ideas on success in the following psalms.

SUCCESS

You are my rock and fortress
The Lord of all my success
Spirit, soul, and body, you want my best
Your Word, I'll pursue with zest

When pressure tries my faith
I'll walk in the Word of Grace
You will never leave me in a spot
I'll not allow my harvest to rot

I am the Lord of all your success
In righteous ways you shall dress
Honor, integrity and pureness of heart
Covenant power for a successful start.

To be a true success you have to know God's heart.

THE GIVER

The giver is one who knows my heart
Giving of themselves is a righteous start
Fulfilling the conditions they have heard
Reaping the promises of My Word

The rut of poverty they shall not see
Their giving will excel throughout eternity
Of My ways they have heard
Reaping the promises of My Word

The giver is somebody who touches my heart
Tithes and offerings is only a start
The love of God they have heard
Reaping the promises of My Word.

My journey in life never really consisted of anybody I could call father or dad. I had a step-father that tried to do right to the best of his abilities. Unfortunate thing for him was he was suddenly a step father to someone else's children at the ripe old age of forty-five. He tried his best and I will give him that. But one thing that was consistent in my life was my mother. My mother is in heaven now enjoying the presence of Jesus and my step-father who gave his life to Jesus just before he died. Mom this psalm is for you.

MOTHER

Patient and gentle she does stand
Kindness and grace are hers to command
Peace and contentment with no strife
She lives a quiet and Godly life

In wisdom and knowledge she does grow

With gentle words she helps us to know
The guidance to fulfill our lives part
Love comes from the depths of her heart

Power and strength to radiate
Disobedience she does hate
A gift of heaven she is from
I'll look forward to calling her... MOM.

In this day and age trouble abounds and hearts are hard. What can be said about you?

TEARS ON A SHOULDER

The tears on your shoulder are there for a reason
The person who left them there was expressing emotion
Joy or sorrow, who can say,
What the emotion of the day

The real question I have to ask
The shoulder cried on is it a task
Many will be bothered by the tear

The color on my sweater is smeared

Are you full of love fulfilling your part?
Your shoulder, a place for others to lay their heart
Satisfaction will be yours I can say
When on your shoulder hearts can lay

We are living in the closing period of the end times with the soon return of Jesus.

THE RIDER

In the clouds O so high
Comes a rider from the sky
On a powerful steed standing true
A resurrected King comes to you

The Word of God is His name
A two edged sword proceeds from the same
Behold the greatness of His power
To bring judgment in that hour

All you who stand to mock
Prepare to be crushed by the Rock

To you who rejoice at His command
Resurrection life will cause you to stand

The book of revelation talks about two suppers. My question to you friend is what supper are you going to attend?

THE SUPPER OF THE LAMB

A banqueting table, the supper of the Lord
A place of honor or judgment with the sword
Blessing and glory and honor and power
Or judgment in that final hour

Blessings at the marriage supper of the Lamb
A place of honor for the worshippers of the "I Am"
The birds that fly in the midst of heaven
Dine on meat with no leaven

Rejoice, the marriage of the Lamb
Servants arrayed in the linen of the "I Am"
Out of His mouth goes a sharp sword
To strike the ungodly horde

The supper of the Lamb! Let us rejoice

A great choir all of one voice
Hide us from the wrath of the Lamb
We are enemies of the "I Am"

The question is to you my friends
Which stanza to you to send
A child of the great "I Am"
Or an enemy of the Lamb?

My desire when it is all said and done is to stand in the throne room of my Father God and join in with the countless angels and saints to give praise and worship to the most high. I enjoy and even crave for His presence and one day it will be permanent.

THRONEROOM

A voice majestically does sound
Thunder and lightning's all around
Twenty four elders clothed in white
Seven lamps burning bright

The living creatures O what a sight
Crying Holy, Holy day and night
Thousands of angels all around
All together with one sound

Worthy, worthy is the Lamb
Power and Honor to the I am
Blessing and honor, glory and power
To the Lamb in that grand hour

We are all on a journey through this life. Many people look for the destination and are so focused on it they don't enjoy the journey. People at times ask how your day is. This question does not get answered truthfully, because if it was answered truthfully most not all would answer according to their emotional state at the moment. Through my life and the anointing (teaching) not to answer most questions emotionally. I am on a journey and I have adventures every day. If I go to sleep in peace then I have conquered the day with its adventure. If I am not in peace then the day is not done until I put my head on my pillow with peace flowing through my heart and soul.

JOURNEY TO THE DESTINATION

Many look and see the destination
They run but only to be disappointed
They fail to realize the organization
Of what they see is time appointed

The journey they fail to see
Is what prepares them for eternity?
The journey the great adventures and joy
Is troubling but trust me emotions not a toy
The journey builds character and strength
The destination takes away my breath
The joy the journey those received
The destination a supernatural rift

This has been my journey as a psalmist for approximately twenty-eight years. It is by no means over. It seems that a person goes through dry spells then a spiritual flood of activity. In the following sections I will continue to share my journey. Not as a psalmist but as a member of the five-fold ministry. I pray the psalms written here will be a source of encouragement to you and even revelation to how much God cares and desires your ultimate success.

THE CALL

Unknown to me the Holy Spirit was planning a supernatural visitation as soon as the household had retired for the night. Well into the early hours of the morning a light illuminating the interior of our house awakened me. Something was drawing me to the source of the light. As I walked into the kitchen I realized the light started outside radiating in. I was compelled into the porch and outside to the steps. The most marvelous sight I had ever seen appeared in the sky above me. A large pair of hands appeared in the sky held together in prayer. The hands began to open and a bible appeared. This bible was so huge it seemed to fill the entire sky. I stood in awe as a passage of scripture was circled.

The scripture was Ezekiel 3:10-11, "Moreover He said to me: "Son of man, receive into your heart all my words that I speak to you, and hear with your ears. And go, get to the captives, to the children of your people, and speak to them and tell them, 'Thus says the Lord God,' whether they hear, or whether they refuse."

After a minute or so of watching this scene I was translated to the far end of my stepfather's grain field. My brothers and sisters were with me. We were standing beside the flat top hay wagon when Jesus appeared. He was wearing royal purple robes and radiated the most brilliant light I had ever seen. The glory radiating from Christ was so brilliant that creation ceased to exist, all you could see was Jesus and His glory, and nothing else was visible.

Jesus stood before us, His hand extended to us. In His hand was a piece of fruit of some sort. He presented this fruit to us, we all stood staring not sure what to do. I took the fruit from His hand and stood in amazement looking at this fruit, as it was not like anything we had ever seen. I decided to take a bite of the fruit. As soon as I bit off a piece of the fruit, the vision ended, I was sitting on the edge of my bed, daylight pouring in through the windows, wondering about the events that just took place.

I never really understood that vision as a child, but one thing was very clear to me; from that time on I wanted to be a minister of the Gospel of Jesus Christ. Life continued on for a young child, school during the week, work on the farm and Sunday school during the weekends. This lifestyle continued until I was fifteen and puberty set in and I experienced a new revelation. Girls now becoming young women, they were no longer funny looking boys to throw mud at and make fun of, but someone you wanted to impress in the worst way.

I moved out of home and to my uncle's house as my family was falling apart. My mother and step father were having marriage problems and would eventually divorce. I spent the next few years travelling around British Columbia, Alberta and Saskatchewan. I found a beautiful woman and married her and had a son. We were in the process of settling down to a quiet life and raising children. Christianity and religion was not part of our life even though my wife had mentioned that she used to go to Sunday school when she was a little girl.

We had what we thought was a normal Canadian lifestyle, full time job with a pay-cheque every two weeks, then a time of relaxation partying with friends. My cousin Victor showed up one evening while we had a small party going on and he asked my wife and me if we would baby sit his son while him and his wife went out for a time of relaxation. We agreed and Victor asked if he could talk to me privately, sure I said. We went into the bedroom and he began to tell me about Jesus, His soon return and end of the age. I would just nod at him and say something like oh yeah okay just to get him out because I wanted to get back to my party.

Victor came by many times to tell me about Jesus return and the end of the age. You know the crazy thing about it was; victor may have been doing a great job of sharing the gospel, but all I heard was, "Jesus is coming back and the earth is going to blow up and we are all going to die."

The spring of 1982 was a turning
Point in my life, which would
Also affect the lives of others around me.
Little did I realize that though?
I walked away from Jesus; HE never walked away from me. In April of 1982 Jesus visited me for the second time. This Visitation caused me to return to the Lord Jesus Christ with a fervent zealousness that still continues in my heart today.

The visitation started with the following scenes taking place: My fellow workers from the muffler shop and I were partying at a Southern American colonial style mansion. There was an abundance of drinking and carousing. I was participating fully when all of a sudden something started to bother my spirit. I did not understand what was happening, but I knew I had to ask God to forgive me for the lifestyle I had indulged in. Seeking privacy, I exited to a balcony overlooking a garden. I started to repent and tell God that I was sorry when I heard a voice say, "Forget it" I was startled and looked around to see who was playing a joke on me. Not finding anyone I continued to ask God's forgiveness. Again I heard a voice say, "Forget it." I looked around a second time, finding no one. This time I was compelled to look into the sky. As I watched the sky an amazing thing happened.

A strange but beautiful presence surrounded me as I watched the clouds change shapes. The clouds changed into a variety of different animals. A voice filled with love and peace spoke from among the animal shaped clouds. In my heart I knew I was talking with God. The voice proceeded to say, "Forget it, I want you to listen to my son Jesus, and if you can't make it grab onto one of the animals and it will bring you to heaven where you belong."[1]

I reached up and grabbed the leg of the closest animal, which happened to be a lamb. Suddenly, I found myself running along a vast expanse of beach. Beautiful, peaceful, and exhilarating was this place was in. I looked out over a huge ocean and was aware that everything I could see was created just for me. I was totally amazed at surroundings, especially the peace I experienced.

Suddenly I was removed from that place and a new scene unfolded before my eyes. I could see a Jesus, standing beside a large rock, watching over his sheep. I walked over to where Jesus was and stood beside him and together we watched the herd of sheep. We watched the sheep together for a little while. We watched in silence not communicating with each other but totally aware of each other. I watched this scene with interest for few minutes. This scene disappeared and I was back at the balcony looking into the sky.

Again the voice of the Lord spoke to me saying, "Forget it, all I want you to do is listen to my Son." At this point I made an unbelieving arrogant statement toward God. Why you might ask would a person make arrogant statements toward God. It is quite simple; being influenced in the occult and street gangs you are taught how to rebel against all authority. To my surprise He responded with authority and sternness, I sensed that if I didn't stop being ignorant my life could be easily finished at that point Even though God responded with sternness the great love He has for His creation never left His voice. Adamantly the Lord said, "LISTEN TO MY SON JESUS." After this statement the visitation ended.

1: Jesus was not telling me to forget about repentance. He was referring to my former lifestyle along with the guilt and fear. By saying forget it He was telling me that He wasn't holding my past against me. The Lord was implying also that I should forget about my past and Follow Jesus.

PHILIPPIANS 3:13-14,

"Brethren, I do not count myself to have apprehended; but one thing I do, forgetting those things which are behind and reaching forward to those things which are ahead, I press toward the goal for the Prize of the upward call of God in Christ Jesus."

At the time of this writing, many events and people have come into my life. I have the sense of being called into two areas of the five-fold ministry, prophet and pastor. Am I a pastoring prophet or a prophetic pastor? I guess time will tell as I trust the Holy Spirit to confirm His call upon my life.

CONFIRMATION OF THE CALL

I believe the year was 1984 and I had recommitted my life to the Lord in 1982 and my wife accepted Jesus in 1983. We were attending a small Pentecostal church relatively close to our house, more out of convenience than anything.

My wife worked as a chambermaid cleaning hotel rooms and usually had to work some Sundays and couldn't attend church with me on a regular basis. I went to church as usual, not knowing that this day was going to be a pivotal day to change the course of my life. As I am writing this I just had the thought, "how many times do we have divine appointments in life that God has ordained to help us fulfill our destinies in Christ, and are totally unaware of them?" I was about to have such a divine appointment.

A little background information before I continue. At this time of my life diplomacy and kindness were not strong personality traits dominate in my life. These traits would be developed later in my life. Anyways I went to church by myself that Sunday as my wife had to work. I sat quietly listening to the message and just like most saints in the church was glad for the closing prayer.

I stood up to leave and a native girl grabbed my arm and very rudely told me, not asked, but told me quite authoritatively that I was taking her home and coming in for a coffee. I was intrigued because no one talked to me like that because I would normally respond in like manner saying something like " who do you think you are ordering me around like that and I have better things to do!"

But nevertheless I said yes ma'am and drove her home and went into her home, which just happened to be the basement duplex my wife and I moved out of a month earlier. She introduced herself as Wynne and proceeded to make coffee while introducing me to her two children. Her and her husband and children had moved to Grande Prairie for work. Grande Prairie has always been a busy town for work. The saying around here was if you're not working it's because you don't want to. Back in those days it seemed like you could go to one business and apply for a job and if the owner didn't meet your requirements you could go next door and get the pay and conditions you wanted.

Wynne and I began to talk about spiritual things, sharing our testimonies on the new birth. I became intrigued when she shared about the manifestations of the Holy Spirit and she was with a group of prayer warriors in her home town in central Alberta who had manifestations of Jesus in their lives.

Wow I was hooked and wanted to know more because I had dreams and open visions of Jesus when I was younger. It was a relief to find someone I could talk to about my experiences who wouldn't respond to me after sharing, "How much drugs did you take the night before?"

Wynne started talking about a subject I had little knowledge of," THE HOLY SPIRIT. "She asked me if I had been baptized with the Holy Spirit with the evidence of speaking in tongues." I proceeded to share with her sensing the presence of God many times and the open visions of Jesus and angels. I shared with her the trances the Holy Spirt gave me showing me His great love for me. As far as I was concerned I was baptized with the Holy Spirit. I was convinced by the Baptist religion I grew up in that you got everything including the Holy Spirit when you accepted Jesus as your savior. Speaking in tongues and miracles all ceased after apostle Paul died because they were needed then because the church was just birthed in the earth and needed something to show that they were of God.

Any speaking in tongues today was a false sign and not of God. I really believed speaking in tongues was of the devil and I loved Jesus so much that I would have no part of a devilish deed. This I did not know was part of the cessation doctrine that says all the manifestations of the Holy Spirit stopped because we have the King James Version of the bible. They use 1 Corinthians 13:10 when that which is perfect is come, then that which is in part shall be done away. They use this scripture to justify why they have no power or manifestations of God in their midst. This is definitely a doctrine of devils meant to keep the church weak and powerless and at the mercy of the devil.

2 Timothy 3:5King James Version (KJV)

⁵ Having a form of godliness, but denying the power thereof: from such turn away.

I did a google search and found the churches that are lacking in manifestations of the Holy Spirit are in decline while the churches that have manifestations of the Holy Spirit are growing.

But enough of the rabbit trail let's get back to Wynne. I presented my arguments to her justifying my position. She wouldn't back down, she stood eyeball to eyeball nose to nose fang to fang with me telling me that I wasn't baptized by the Holy Spirit but I was operating under the counsel of the Holy Spirit. Seeing she was a formidable foe whom I could not get to back down I graciously excused myself saying that I had to pick my wife up from work. When I got in my vehicle and drove about a block away I spoke really loud to God saying, "IF I DON'T HAVE THE HOLY SPIRIT I WANT HIM BECAUSE I WANT EVERYTHING YOU HAVE FOR ME."

I arrived at the hotel where my wife worked and explained to her that I met a really strange and unique woman at church today and she needed to meet her. We drove back to Wynne's house and I introduced the two women, they clicked right away and became fast friends. Wynne's husband worked out of town and she enjoyed the company. We continued to fellowship on a biweekly basis, learning about prophecy and other manifestations of the Holy Spirit. One evening she asked us if we were interested in a hallelujah party. We asked her what that was. She told us that we would go into the front room and begins to praise and worship God until He manifested in our midst. I never heard of such a thing. Sure we sing songs of worship and praise in church but that was out of duty and the program we are taught. A couple of fast songs then a couple of slow songs, an offering, then a forty-five minute sermon, which may or may not put you to sleep. Then the most anticipated moment of the whole Sunday church service came, the closing prayer and dismissal for lunch.

Wow praise God until He showed up, I was enticed wondering if it would work and how long would you actually have to praise and worship. We moved into the front room and began to sing praise songs and proclaim the blood of Jesus. After about half an hour I felt this peaceful presence enter the room, soothing warmth began to cover my head and flow down the back of my neck. My mind quickly turned off all natural thoughts and I could see Jesus walk into the room in my mind's eye.

Wynne moved beside my wife and asked her if she wanted to be baptized with the Holy Spirit. She said yes and Wynne laid hands on her and began to pray. Something unusual happened, my wife began to laugh. Every time Wynne would pray for her to receive the baptism of the Holy Spirit my wife would always break out in laughter. That wasn't the expected result. The bible gives us guide lines that we are to expect and follow.

Acts 2:4 ⁴ and they were all filled with the Holy Spirit and began to speak in other tongues as the Spirit gave them utterance.

The Holy Spirit Falls on the Gentiles

Acts 10:44 while Peter was still saying these things, the Holy Spirit fell on all who heard the word. ⁴⁵ And the believers from among the circumcised who had come with Peter were amazed, because the gift of the Holy Spirit was poured out even on the Gentiles.

⁴⁶ For they were hearing them speaking in tongues and extolling God.

Acts 19: And when Paul had laid his hands on them, the Holy Spirit came on them, and they began speaking in tongues and prophesying.

I admitted that I had some misbeliefs about God but when I read the truth in the bible, GOD'S WORD, my belief system changed. I also found out another truth.

Acts 10:34 King James Version (KJV)

³⁴ Then Peter opened his mouth, and said, of a truth I perceive that God is no respecter of persons:

If God not being a respecter of persons baptized the apostles and the early church with the Holy Spirit with evidence of speaking in tongues then He will do the same for us today.

Luke 3:16 King James Bible
John answered, saying unto *them* all, I indeed baptize you with water; but one mightier than I cometh, the latchet of whose shoes I am not worthy to unloose: he shall baptize you with the Holy Ghost and with fire:

Matthew 3:11 New International Version
"I baptize you with water for repentance. But after me comes one who is more powerful than I, whose sandals I am not worthy to carry. He will baptize you with the Holy Spirit and fire.

Mark 1:8 King James Bible
I indeed have baptized you with water: but he shall baptize you with the Holy Ghost.

I am not greater than the apostles or the early church declaring that I don't need what they had. I need the Holy Spirit and His manifestations more today than ever before. We are living in the closing hours of the last days and sin is increasing and putting pressure on the body of Christ like never before.

The Holy Spirit is preparing the Body of Christ for a supernatural end time harvest of souls and needs your participation in this event. Throw away the deception and misbeliefs that Satan has convinced you of and take the bible literally and watch the results.

As I was saying my wife would break out laughing every time Wynne prayed for her. We decided to let it be and move on. We continued to praise God and enjoy His presence, having bouts of laughter for no reason whatsoever but really enjoying the overwhelming sensation of God's love.

Feeling tired we decided to shut it down for the night and maybe fast and pray for answers as to why my wife would break out in laughter every time hands were laid on her to receive the Holy Spirit. We started the praise about 10-10:30 pm and thought must be about midnight, time to go home and sleep. When we looked at the clock it was 3:30 am. Wow we were praising and enjoying the presence of the Lord for five hours, magnificent. We quickly got hooked on hallelujah parties and wanted more. A week later we got together again. We had spent the week fasting and praying while doing our daily activities. When we got together this time we were very focused in our praise and prayer. Last time being beginners we just shot everything out there hoping God would show up. He did because of His great Love for His children. We were baby Christians running around in our spiritual pampers so to speak.

    As we praised and prayed the Holy Spirit showed up and a word of knowledge manifested. The reason for the blockage was because of my wife's involvement in the occult that was never repented of. When my wife talked about it she usually had a look of satisfaction knowing that she could lift a two hundred fifty pound man off the floor by placing two fingers under him and lifting straight up with little to no effort. She realized her mistake and repented of the activity and never again had excitement over it but sorrow over it. I had never heard her talk about again. Wynne asked me to lay hands on my wife and agree with her in prayer for my wife to receive the Holy Spirit. As soon as I laid my hands on my wife I started speaking in tongues, a German sounding dialect.

I received without asking because my heart became open to Him because of what I read in the bible. My wife received the Holy Spirit and spoke in tongues that evening as well. We stayed in the presence of the Lord for many hours. We decided to stay at Wynne's house upon her request for the weekend and enjoy the fellowship and hallelujah parties. The next night and hallelujah party would be a turning point in my life. We fellowshipped and enjoyed the days adventure having a late supper finishing around 10:00pm. We decided to finish our coffee and go into the living room at about 11:00pm and start praise to our magnificent God. About an hour into worship the presence of God was so strong your hair could stand up by itself. The word of wisdom and the word of knowledge began to flow through prophecy. Let's just say the Holy Spirit was in manifestation through the revelation gifts.

    The Word the Lord was spoken over me that I was called into the office of a prophet and that God was going to gift me and prepare me to fulfill my destiny. I received this word with joy and excitement not knowing what a prophet is and does, just thinking if this is from God it has to be good. **GOD IS GOOD ALWAYS AND IN ALL WAYS GOD IS GOOD.**

I looked out the window and realized we were in the presence of the Lord all night. The sun was starting to come up and I decided to go outside for fresh air. I went outside and stood on the sidewalk by my car. A very gentle breeze began to gust gently. I was amazed as to what I could hear with each gentle gust. I could hear the name of Jesus spoken very gently and drawn out, **JJJJEEEESSSSUUUUSSSS.** As each gust came by I would hear the name of Jesus spoken in the same sweet drawn out manner. This continued on for about fifteen minutes. Needless I was excited and ran into the house to share my experience only to find everybody went to sleep after the night of worship.

I tried to sleep but to no avail. I was pumped up excited and wondering what manifestation of the Holy Spirit was that? I think I figured it out that it was a revelation gift, knowing that there may be 9 manifestations of the Holy Spirit, but you can categorize them in three different categories.

1. THE POWER GIFTS
A. GIFT OF FAITH
B. GIFTS OF HEALINGS
C. WORKING OF MIRACLES
2. REVELATION GIFTS
A. WORD OF KNOWLEDGE
B. WORD OF WISDOM
C. DISCERNING OF SPIRITS
3. THE SPEAKING GIFTS
A. SPEAKING IN TONGUES
B. INTERPRETATION OF TONGUES
C. PROPHECY

Regardless of the category, I think people can get caught up into analyzing God to the point of missing the experience. I believe the Holy Spirit gave me this experience maybe just to show that He loved me and knew I would be tickled pink by it and would always remember it with pleasure and adonization for Him.

2 Corinthians 13:14 Berean Study Bible
May the grace of the Lord Jesus Christ, and the love of God, and the fellowship of the Holy Spirit be with all of you. Out of that experience this poem or psalm as I would like to call them was written.

NATURE

The birds, flowers and trees do sing
Rejoicing in the Lord their melodies ring
Watching the sun about half past five
When all of a sudden the breeze was alive

As the breeze continued on bye
The name of Jesus was exalted on high
As the anointing began to flow
A new revelation for me to know

Then one day while reading the Word
All excited over the phrase I heard
Sun, moon and stars of light
Praise His name this very night.

As I began to read my bible, especially the Old Testament about prophets, I was beginning to think, can we talk about this calling. I found the prophet's ministry interesting and a bit exciting but the no failure; no mistake rule was a bit disturbing. Regardless of the non-error allowed rule when you got it right people didn't like you and tried to hurt you. I realized the first time I mentioned this call to a person I looked up to and got " TELL ME SOMETHING THAT IS GOING TO HAPPEN IN THE NEAR FUTURE AND YOU BETTER BE RIGHT." I learned real quickly that the prophet's ministry was not really accepted so keep it quiet what God is doing in your life. I decided the best thing for me to do was to research this calling and ministry out for myself.

I read a scripture that gave me confidence in this matter and prayed for confirmation to this call of the office of the prophet.

2 Corinthians 13:1 Berean Study Bible this is the third time I am coming to you. "Every matter must be established by the testimony of two or three witnesses."

I prayed in my heart, "I don't know enough of this ministry and calling so I will wait for you to confirm it by two or three people who have never met and have no idea of each other." While I am waiting I will search this ministry out with all available sources at my disposal. I searched and searched and would only come across little pieces of information that gave some insight but would cause more questions. I did get my confirmations a few years later. The second confirmation came from the two spiritual fathers I had who ordained me. I never told them about my call from the dream I had when I was ten years old or from Wynne. When they ordained me they publically announced their belief that God had called me into the office of a prophet. But before that happened let me share a rather humorous story of the first time I prophesied.

I had been learning how to hear the voice of God in the mornings during prayer time.

John 10:27New King James Version (NKJV)

²⁷ My sheep hear my voice, and I know them, and they follow me.

I would get up around 5-6 am and go into the front room and pray. I would usually start with something like this. "Good morning Father, how's heaven today"? Then I would proceed to pray for king and country, my family and relatives and church meetings and anything else that would come across my mind. I continued this way for about a week. One morning I just got past my greeting of "Good morning Father how's heaven?" When I heard so loud in my spirit that I thought heard it audible with my ears. "HEAVENS GREAT HOW'S EARTH?" I was stunned into silence thinking how's earth? You are the all present all powerful all-knowing God and you ask me how's earth?

He knew my thoughts and said "I am talking to you the same way you are talking to me."

Wow, what a revelation, the God of the universe desires to fellowship with us that He temporarily sets aside His awesomeness in order to fellowship with us on our level. He approaches us where we are at but has a desire to raise us up eventually to His level. You may say impossible, yes with man but not with God. Anyways hearing god in private but speaking on His behalf in the form of a prophecy is totally out there and scary to me.

Sitting in the church one Sunday morning I noticed we had an unusual anointing on the praise and worship which was exciting. About half way through the worship I started hearing words down in my spirit and I instinctively knew I was to start repeating them when there was a break in the music. I began to argue with the Holy Spirit which lasted less than a couple of seconds but in my mind seemed like an hour.

I reminded the Holy Spirit who the pastor was, a one man show and everything was about him and I would probably get disciplined and maybe kicked out of the church. The Holy Spirit told me to say what He told me to say or He would make me stand up and apologize to the congregation that I had a word from the Lord and I refused to give it.

    Hahaha, you are thinking "God wouldn't do that, make you apologize." Have you forgotten what I mentioned about myself earlier? Diplomacy and kindness were not yet part of my development yet. The Holy Spirit knows how to get through to me to accomplish His will. I began to repeat the words I heard. I never got a paragraph or a book at once I just got a word and as I spoke each word another just fell off of my lips. It was an encouraging word of God's love and favour for the congregation. Something was taking place in that congregation I had never seen before, a freedom was erupting as a woman began to sing in tongues to my right another behind me interpreted the tongue sang in and another person started prophesying about the goodness of God. The place was a Holy Ghost fire pit and I chuckled to myself thinking "Thank you Jesus, he can't throw us all out." I learned a lot about walking in obedience in that situation. My family eventually moved to another Pentecostal church in town that was known for moving in the manifestations of the Holy Spirit.

Let's get back to the confirmation of two or three witnesses. The second witness was a revivalist from Saskatchewan. We had a few meetings with him the year before and it seemed everything was about laughter. You get half way through a message and the congregation would burst out laughing. Not one here or there everybody would just burst out laughing. The praise and worship was phenomenal, the congregation wouldn't stop. The pastor would have to interrupt so the guest speaker could share the message God wanted to say for those revival meetings that were taking place in the late 90's. This revivalist came back early 2001 or so and we had another intense meeting. It wasn't so much laughter as before but more serious talking of a great awakening coming to the world and revival coming to a sleepy church.

He would call people out of the congregation, prophecy over them or pray for healing after a word of knowledge. The people were blessed and encouraged to continue in the faith no matter what they were going through. I was watching the events rejoicing with those who rejoiced and pleased that God was meeting the needs of the people. Suddenly he called me up and told me to raise my arms which I obeyed and he barely touched my forehead and the Spirit of God enveloped me and I fell forward into his arms. The ushers grabbed me and laid me on the floor and the most unusual vision unfolded. I found myself sitting with my back to a tree. This tree wasn't in the middle of a forest but sitting in an open meadow. This was a fruit tree of some kind, not like an apple or other hard type of fruit, but a soft fruit that you could squeeze it with your fingers and it would almost liquefy as it ran through your fingers.

    Jesus was sitting on the other side of the tree in contemplation. He stood up and had a broad smile on His face and plucked a piece of fruit from the tree. Jesus continued to walk around the tree to where I was sitting. As He got closer to me He began to chuckle harder and louder. In the vision I could hear my thoughts of wonderment, is it a riddle or a joke or a humorous story Jesus is going to tell me while we are sharing this fruit together? By this time Jesus was standing in front of me laughing and He bent down slightly as to sit beside me I thought when He did the most unexpected thing I could imagine. He squashed the soft fruit in my face and rubbed it in as it poured down my face. Then as quickly as the vision started it ended with that scenario. I picked myself off the floor and made my way back to my chair and sat down mystified to as what I had just seen.

After a few minutes and the revivalist ministering to a few more people called on me. "William, come up here come up here." I obeyed and proceeded to the front again. I stood in front of him and he told me to raise my hands and asked if I was ready? I said yes and thought to myself he will touch me and I will go down and maybe Jesus will explain that previous vision to me. He asked me again, "are you ready?" I said yes. He then told me to raise my hands higher. I did what he asked only to get asked again, "Are you ready?" Feeling a bit annoyed because I wanted to get back to that tree and have Jesus explain the vision to me. That of course is what I wanted to happen and thought it would. I was expecting a touch on the forehead like before and everyone else when came another totally unexpected thing like Jesus and the fruit. The revivalist open handed slapped me across the face with such force that I did a three sixty and landed on the floor on my face with no catchers catching me because they never seen that coming either. I was on the floor enveloped in a white cloud when the revivalist kneeled down and began to speak in a loud voice that God has called William Hatfield into the office of a prophet and that He, God was going to show His Glory through my face.

Wow that not only explains the vision but gives me another confirmation of the call on my life. Okay now I am kind of excited thinking now I know why I am born and my purpose. Time to intensify my research of the prophet's ministry. I was in luck or should say rather blessed to find the church book keeper was running a home Christian book store. I found volumes of books on the prophet's ministry, ordered them and consumed them. One afternoon my friends and I heard of a prophet visiting a little church a couple of hours away from our city. Apparently he prophesied the church he was visiting into existence and named the pastors while the building was a broke down abandoned movie theatre. We went to that church for Sunday afternoon service and it started as church usually does. When the prophet began to speak it was an upbeat encouraging message. He then paused and pointed to my friends and told them things about their lives and children, which I can say at the time of this writing all has been fulfilled. He then continued with his sermon. After about ten minutes he points to me and says, you have been called into the office of a prophet and you have a great ability to do research and God is going to use you to raise the dead.

    Another confirmation to the call on my life. I pretty well settled the issue and decided to research and study and learn about the prophets ministry. I went to Bible College because they had a course on the prophetic. That was the only course of interest. I studied pastoral theology and the other courses seemed tedious to me. The college had a test to show character traits which showed what ministry your personality makeup is best suited for. I scored 100% on prophet/perceiver and 100% on teacher and 85% on giver. I think I scored 60% or less for pastor. Even in the bible college the assistant dean recognized the prophet's ministry on my life. I also noticed the dean of the bible college also mentioned many times that I had a pastor's heart. He had noticed me sitting with other students helping them through issues in their lives. As I said I settled it in my life but I won't run around calling myself prophet because there is a lot of danger in that manly from people's misbeliefs and expectations they force upon you and I like a quiet peaceful life.

    Content to know why I am here on this earth and not interested in fame as I watched some self-proclaimed prophets run after only to find themselves on the scrap heap of life. With all that said and done content to know and now study and learn to show myself a workman in the kingdom.

2 Timothy 2:15 New King James Version (NKJV)

¹⁵ Be diligent to present yourself approved to God, a worker who does not need to be ashamed, rightly dividing the word of truth.

Off to church I go not aware there is a special speaker from Alaska today. I was at this time running the sound board in church. The sound board was in the balcony where I could see the whole front of the church. This speaker was not the same old breed that we usually have and are today. It is hard to break out of our same old same format we have used for centuries in the church. Instead of having a sermon this speaker from Alaska began ministering in the Spirit immediately. Let me encourage you, this minister even though he had no sermon to preach ministered by the Spirit within the confines of the scripture. You could quote scripture for every prophecy and ministry he did to individuals. After a few minutes he looked up to the balcony and called me down. As I walked down the aisle he says "do you know why you are going through all the troubles and trials in your life? It is to get you out of the way because you are called into the office of a prophet and there can't be anything of you in that office only God through you." Icing on the cake, another confirmation but filling in the blanks to a lot of questions.

All these confirmations came in after Wynne and her family had moved east to Ontario. They had no knowledge of her and she them nor did they know each other. Let me say something to you who may be called into the prophet's ministry. The prophet is gender neutral meaning it is an office that can be filled by either sex same as the teacher and evangelist. The only offices reserved for men are the apostle and prophet which have masculine connotations in their meanings, and in the Greek both mean father. We see no evidence of female pastor or apostle in the New Testament. Anyways there is an order to the prophet's ministry. First the call which may be a supernatural dream like I had or maybe another prophet laid hands on you and declared that office to you. Just because you have the call doesn't make you the great prophet of God's man or woman of the hour. Second is the anointing which is the training period. This training period could take up to fifteen to twenty years depending on you and the area of ministry you will be released in. Third is the appointing when you will be released by the Holy Spirit to flow in the gifts placed in your life. God will confirm His Word spoken through your mouth with signs and wonders. Until then you are still in the anointing stage so just relax and grow. Don't be impatient you will get there when the time is right and you are ready. Too soon and you will get hurt. We are all still in training and will never be out until after we are home with Jesus.

Don't overlook the people who come across your path for it may be a divine appointment needed to get you back on destinies trail. Let me recap;

1. The call when I was ten.
2. Wynne prophesying the call
3. Spiritual fathers ordained the call
4. Revivalist declaring the call with signs
5. Prophet speaking the call with wonders
6. The Alaskan declaring the call with trials
7. Heeding the call and let's enter the anointing stage of growth and training to be all that God called me to be.

I have discussed point 6 with some people and they have a hard time believing it. In Acts 9:16 New International Version (NIV)

[16] I will show him how much he must suffer for my name."

I know this is talking about the apostle Paul and I by no means put myself on the same level as the apostle Paul. However I believe that if you are called of God into an effective ministry of building the kingdom of God and destroying the works of Satan, there will be trials. If Satan gets knowledge of the call I am sure he will do everything in his power to stop it. Anyways this is my story and I am sharing it to possibly give hope and understanding to many that may be going through similar situations in life.

>May you find joy in your journey to find the call on your life? May the peace of God consume you as you seek Him?

THE ANOINTING

1 john 2: **20** King James Version, But ye have an unction from the Holy One, and ye know all things.
1 john 2:20 New International Version: But you have an anointing from the Holy One, and all of you know the truth.
New International Version
 1 john 2:27 as for you, the anointing you received from him remains in you, and you do not need anyone to teach you. But as his anointing teaches you about all things and as that anointing is real, not counterfeit--just as it has taught you, remain in him.

King James Bible
1 john 2:27 But the anointing which ye have received of him abideth in you, and ye need not that any man teach you: but as the same anointing teacheth you of all things, and is truth, and is no lie, and even as it hath taught you, ye shall abide in him.

Firstly, what does it mean to *anoint*, the *anointing* or to be *anointed*? There are many Hebrew and Greek words in relation to anointing. But for the sake of study, I will only mention a few.

Anoint:
-Hebrew - verb
Mashach: To rub with oil, to consecrate and to paint.
Cwk: Pronounce 'sook': To smear over.
-Greek
Murizoz: To apply (unguent).

The Basic meaning of the word anoint is simply to *smear something on an object.*

Usually oil is involved, but it could be other substances such as paint or dye. This gives the idea that to anoint something or someone is an act of consecration.

-Hebrew - <u>noun</u>
Mashyach: 'anointed one' one who is consecrated for a special office or function?

In simple terms, the anointing is the presence of the Holy Spirit being smeared upon someone. It is the overflowing life of Jesus which imparts supernatural strength enabling an individual to perform a special task or function in an office he is called and appointed to.

In simple layman's terms you cannot be taught legalistically to flow in any kind of ministry form. I know people who take 1 John 2:20, 27 and think that they don't have to go to church or bible study because God will teach them. These people usually come up with revelations so far off from the bible they end up wearing the label of fruit cakes and do more harm to the Christian faith than good.

Ephesians 4: [11] So Christ himself gave the apostles, the prophets, the evangelists, the pastors and teachers, [12] to equip his people for works of service, so that the body of Christ may be built up [13] until we all reach unity in the faith and in the knowledge of the Son of God and become mature, attaining to the whole measure of the fullness of Christ.

We have the fivefold ministry to help us grow up. To say we don't need them because I have an anointing is to reject the very word of God that declares that Jesus gave us them.

I am going to try to explain in anointing in my own words, how I understand it. There is nothing about the fivefold minister's that are like a form letter. Every church group is unique and they need a pastor who fits their temperament. The pastor has an anointing from God to work with the congregation to bring them to the fullness of Christ.

I believe the same thing goes for the prophet's ministry. We have local prophets, regional prophets, provincial prophets, prophets to the country and prophets to the earth. One prophet heralds the first coming of Jesus to a nation of Israel. There will be thousands of prophets heralding the second coming of Jesus to the earth. If God called you he will anoint you to teach you how to operate within the call. You cannot fulfill a spiritual call by natural means. To be honest it's not your great self that will stand before the judgment seat of Christ bragging about your great deeds you have performed in the flesh or natural realm. The person who stands before God willing to yield their lives to the Holy Spirit to be used in whatever area He wishes will receive the greatest rewards.

Matthew 10:39 King James Bible
He that findeth his life shall lose it: and he that loseth his life for my sake shall find it.

    Okay let's continue; I have watched people make up prophecies, copy other's prophetic words and regurgitate them hoping they will pass off for a prophetic person or maybe a prophet. This is silliness at its finest. You may get away with it temporarily but when the crunch comes, push to shove you will be revealed because you will have to stand by yourself. When your sponge is squeezed what's in there will come out and your true self will emerge. Are you truly called, or a copycat, or a wannabe hoping to fake it until you make it. I have met people in these areas and they just give the prophetic and prophet's ministries, which are ordained of God to bless, edify and encourage people, a bad name and a sour taste.

EVIDENCE OF THE ANOINTING

I want to share a series of stories and events that have happened in my life. These events are probably not in chronological order, but in order as I remember them from the mid-eighties until now 2017. I will start with this event since I was just a couple years back serving the Lord. I think but not to be quoted about 1985 and I was learning about spiritual activity. Everything was great when my wife and I retired for the evening; WHEN it seemed like all hell broke loose, partying noise from upstairs, doors opening and closing by themselves, clock making loud ticking sounds after the batteries were out and had no power to function.

Even a mirror lifted off the dresser and crashed against the wall falling to the floor in pieces. When I went to pick up the pieces I heard an audible voice say "touch those and I will cut your throat." Needless to say I backed off and decided to put a praise cassette to calm everything down. I mentioned partying upstairs; we have no tenants living in our attic.

I had learned that praise and worship puts the enemy to flight so put on a praise cassette and everything should be fine. I was expecting everything to stop when the cassette began to speed up and the music became garbled. Fear engulfed me, my hair stood up and I grabbed my family and ran out of the house. I did not want anything to do with a haunted house. We went to my Cousin Victor's house and told him the story.

Victor smiled and said okay let's go to your place and do something about it. My wife and children were spending the rest of the night so they are safe. I tried to back pedal because honestly I was scared and wanted nothing to do with that situation. My cousin, the big brave lion heart, would not let me alone, we are going. I agreed and when we got into the driveway I said, "You go first and turn on the lights and I will follow you." When we got to the door he said "the devil attacked you in the dark we are going to fight him in the dark." I thought you are welcome to do it and when you are done come get me I will be waiting in your car. I followed Victor into the house and down stairs to the basement. He began to quote scripture and take authority over the devil and plead the blood of Christ over the house.

I noticed that there was no retaliation from the enemy like I thought there might be. After all when you watched the movies the monsters and demons eventually lost but the good guys suffered wounds and maybe a fatality or two and I thought I was sure to be a fatality. After a few minutes there was peace in the basement so we headed upstairs where all the heavy activity occurred earlier. I was getting fear free and boldness came upon me as I followed my cousin. We continued to plead the blood of Christ when something extraordinary happened. I could see into the spirit realm and seen the devil or demon that had being causing problems in my house. It was about 5ft 7in skinny and ugly looking. To my surprise it was hiding in the hall closet and shaking like it was scared.

I mentioned this to Victor and he came up with a plan of attack, attack and not retreat, the boldness was increasing exponentially. I would grab the closet door swing it open and he would lunge in and attack the demon. Side note: Victor brought with him his big family bible which must have weighed a good fifteen pounds. We got into position, I am holding the hall door handle and Victor in front of the door with the bible held over his head in an attack position. Our adrenalin was flowing as we were anticipating a massive free for all fight. Victor said okay and I pulled the door open with so much force that it almost came off the hinges. When I pulled it open something came out of the closet and victor lunged at it beating it with his words of rebuke and repeatedly hitting it with his big bible.

Satisfied we were victorious and no demon would ever come near that house again but give warnings to his fellow demons to avoid that property unless they wanted to get a bad beating. We turned on the lights; remember we were doing this spiritual warfare in the dark. The light came on and revealed the item that fell out of the closet when I almost tore the door off its hinges. It was my wife's ironing board. Victor was rebuking and beating my wife's ironing board with his fifteen pound bible. I had to buy a new board for the wife. We looked at each other and giggled but I knew this for a fact I will never be in fear over the activities of the devil again. I had a revelation of the blood of Jesus Christ the most powerful force in existence.

Revelation 12:11 King James Version (KJV)

[11] And they overcame him by the blood of the Lamb and by the word of their testimony; and they loved not their lives unto the death.

Before you judge us let me add that we were baby Christians who put on our big boy pampers and moved out in the revelation we had. I can really put my imagination to work and believe God the Father was watching his two children working together to defeat fear. I can really picture God the Father sitting on his throne and chuckling as Victor rebuked and beat the ironing board with his big bible.

My family and I returned home and found scriptures in the bible dealing with fear and soon conquered fear. The thing that struck me the most out of that was I seen into the spirit realm and knew where that demon was hiding. I believe that was the manifestation of the Holy Spirit called the Discerning of Spirits.

Another time I was in bed and ready to sleep after a tiring day. I closed my eyes and was drifting off to sleep when I sensed the presence of God strong around me. I opened my eyes to take a peek and could see Jesus kneeling by my bed just looking at me with a smile on his face. I just closed my eyes and had the most peaceful sleep in a long time. When I woke up the next morning I was thinking of a scripture I had read earlier that week.

Psalm 3:5 New Living Translation
I lay down and slept, yet I woke up in safety, for the LORD was watching over me.

I was thinking about how I would quietly walk into my sons room and look at him while he slept in his crib and imagine him growing up to do great things and be a person of great influence for the Lord.

One thing I noticed was that a lot of personal encounters happen in the middle of the night. I would wake up after an encounter to look at the clock and notice it is 3-3:30 am.

Again I woke up about 3:00 am to see an angel walking slowly at the end of my bed through my bedroom. I looked at him and asked what are you doing here? He stopped at the end of my bed and stared at me. He said nothing so I asked, "What is your assignment?" He smiled at me and walked through the wall. I thought how rude, he comes into my house and doesn't even say anything just walks through my bedroom. There you go natural carnal thinking to try and understand spiritual situations.

I prayed and asked God what had just happened and why. The Spirit of God said "I am showing you that the gift of Discerning of Spirits is now active in your life." The discerning of spirits is when your eyes are opened up to see in the spirit world. You see Jesus and the angels; you also see demonic entities as well. You can also discern the heart of a man. This gift is desperately needed by the church to protect it from charlatans. Too many Christians fall victim to so called ministers selling green hankies and water from the river Jordan so they can get healed and untold riches. If the believer had the discerning of Spirit active they would reject this silliness, knowing their blessings come from Jesus and not hankies and muddy water supposedly from the river Jordan.

DREAMS

Let's take a look at dreams now. My second spiritual dream happened just shortly after the first one when I see the bible in the sky. This dream involved me flying in an airplane and then suddenly I was outside of the airplane looking in the window. I noticed a black box under the seat. Suddenly the black box exploded and the plane crashed. This dream happened three nights in a row. I never understood the dream but would turn on the evening news to hear about a plane crash with no survivors. I just thought maybe it's a warning not to fly in planes because they are unsafe. It wasn't until a few years later that I began to have understanding of dreams that I figured this one out.

Dreams are parabolic in nature and are not to be taken literally. Flying dreams either in a plane or by yourself represent you being on a spiritual high after an encounter with God. Something dark or black in the dream represents an attack of the devil to rob you of the fullness of your experience. I was being warned that there was an attack coming which did happen and caused me to leave the church for a few years. You can read about it in my first book Repentance before Resurrection. I returned to the Lord through a dream as mentioned earlier in the chapter the call. I have had many dreams since then. One that stands out in my mind is dreaming of running on a large peaceful ocean shore and then diving into the ocean. I stayed under the ocean for what seemed like hours and never had to come up for breath. I swam around with the fishes, whales and sharks in a state of relative peace. I woke

up the next morning thinking maybe God showed me my heavenly home, not the mansion but my back yard. Didn't he say in John 14:3
and, if I go and prepare a place for you, I will come again, and receive you to myself; that where I am, there you may be also. Since He knows how much I like swimming it would only make sense for my mansion in heaven to have an ocean size swimming pool. Again, natural carnal thinking to try and understand spiritual concepts, which didn't work. I believe I was being told that I was going to have a ministry among the nations represented by the ocean. I have been to the Philippines and had good success and have been invited back. I enjoyed the time there and look forward to other countries to minister in. I have had dreams of churches that I have attended. I have attended a few churches after my spiritual father resigned and left his

church to another pastor. I won't name the churches out of respect for them. Just because I don't fit in a particular church doesn't mean you don't. Maybe the reason I don't fit is because of the dream of Jesus and I watching a herd of sheep while standing beside a huge boulder was Him telling me that I will be an under shepherd to Him of our own congregation one day. I am totally open to that as I continue to find my place in the great body of Christ.

Two dreams about one church I was attending started with me wanting a little peace and drove out to a secluded area near a forest. The fresh smell of nature and birds singing was quite relaxing when I noticed two men approaching my car. The man on the passenger side reached in the window and grabbed my sunglasses. The other man came to my driver's door and tried to get in, but I locked it before he got there. I wasn't sure about being alone in the bush with a couple of large threatening men. I started driving away with him hanging from my door yelling he wanted my car. The dream ended. I went to my spiritual father and discussed the dream. The conclusion was the sunglasses represented the vision for my life while the car represented my life. So it was a warning dream that the vision God has given me for my life was in danger of being hijacked. The second dream about this church was I am in a buffet food restaurant with some friends when I noticed the pastor and his wife sitting at a table eating lunch. I excused myself from my friends and went to say hello to the pastor and his wife. When I approached the table I noticed the pastor's wife had a baby in her arms. I was asked to join them so I sat beside the pastor. After a few minutes of conversation the pastor grabbed me by the head and securely planted a kiss on my lips. His wife smiled and chuckled while saying, "you don't know when you are going to be kissed by a friend do you?" that dreams was easy but disturbing to interpret. The kiss was a Judas kiss of betrayal. The wife holding a baby represented the age of the church at the time of betrayal. I then remembered the time I first attended that church. My dreams and visions for ministry meant nothing and I would have to submit my life to their goals and dreams. If I wanted to be a part of their denomination then my dreams would be thrown away because everything was about them and no one else.

That's why we have many church organizations in the body of Christ. Each one has a unique role to fulfill and as believers we have to find where we fit. The last dream of a church was an interesting dream. Not a warning dream like other dreams about being involved in a certain church. I enjoyed attending this particular church, the fellowship was great. I enjoyed the men's group and bible studies we were involved in. I had a reoccurring dream, each one similar to each other but a little twist. The first dream was I was in a suv and driving out of Grande Prairie heading west. In the dream I was aware that I was moving away rather than just going for a drive.

I went to church the next Sunday and shared the dream with a couple of men. Their response was we don't want you to move, you fit right in this church and we enjoy your company. I decided okay I will stay because it after all was just a dream and the dream was to general. If I had an actual destination in the dream rather than west I would have thought differently.

Rabbit trail…. Years earlier I had a dream that I was to move to Guelph Ontario. My wife at the time was watching a program on television about people on the street and prayed "Please send someone to help those people." Little did she realize the Holy Spirit was dealing with me about BE PREPARED TO BE THE ANSWER TO YOUR OWN PRAYERS? I never knew the prayer my wife prayed but started having dreams of ministering to street people. I shared my dreams with my wife and she mentioned the television program and her prayer. Our ministry up to this point had been a coffee table ministry. What I mean by that is sitting in people's homes sharing Jesus over the coffee table or kitchen table. We seemed to attract the kind of people that really never fit in a well-dressed well-groomed setting. Church it seemed to these people was a religious adventure of hypocrites and legalistic judgmental people.

Anyways I dreamed one night the name of the city so we sold everything we could to get finances to go and left with our clothes only and a few ministry items. The crazy thing is we ran out of money before we got there and had to stop at a town many miles from our destination. I went into the social services to see if we could get help and they said no. I responded well I guess we look for a place here and we live here. As soon as I said that they cut me a cheque for a few hundred dollars and we continued our journey. We got to Guelph with little money left and went to a soup kitchen to eat and told them we had nowhere to live and boom we had lodgings for the night. God worked everything out so we lived in a motel room for three months while we ministered to street people. We see people come to Jesus and start a new life. After three months the Holy Spirit said go back west. I thought we were heading back to Grande Prairie when the wheel fell off the utility trailer we were pulling at Saskatoon Saskatchewan. We spent three years in Saskatoon leading bible study and had two years of Bible College. During our time in Saskatoon we saw many hundred people come to Jesus as we ministered to street people, prostitutes and bikers. We eventually ended up back in Grande Prairie for work.

Okay back to the church. I decided to stay because I fit and got along with everyone. About a week later I had another dream of moving but this time I was pulling a U-Haul behind the SUV. I mentioned it again to the men and got the same response. I made the same decision to stay. After a couple of weeks I had a third dream. I was again in a SUV and heading west almost on top of Richmond Hill when I looked in the rear view mirror. In the rear view mirror I could see the Shekinah glory cloud of God settle upon Grande Prairie. In the dream the temptation to turn around was great because wow who wouldn't want to be in the middle of the Glory of God. The Spirit of God spoke loudly to me even if you see this don't go back because I am not there for you. I got the picture, when it is time to move I will go no matter what's happening where I am currently living. I believe the destination is revealed to me through different circumstances. Now that the destination is generally known now when God supplies the finances I will go. Two more dreams I wish to share. One involves spiritual warfare the other may have been a translation, I will leave that for you to decide. The warfare dream actually has its roots in an act of unknown disobedience of an impression I should have listened to.

My wife and I went to bed totally healthy. I started dreaming that a 6ft 6in 250lb person wearing a black robe with a hoody covering his head came in my bedroom. I woke up in the dream to be aware this entity was a demon. I jumped out of bed and started punching him and said get out. I knocked his hoody off to reveal the head of a pig and fangs of a vampire. I said you are an ugly demon and I want you out of here. I continued beating him as the dream ended. I woke up the next morning in severe pain throughout my entire body like I had just been in a bar room brawl. My wife, healthy the night before, was in agony from a sinus headache. I never gave the dream much thought until a few days later. I went to the doctor and he told me that I had rheumatoid arthritis. This dream was about 2001. I made the mistake of agreeing with the doctor and accepting the condition. I accepted the illness claiming it as my own and could only talk sickness. This is the meaning of the dream; the pig head represented an unclean spirit as you can read the Old Testament and see the pig is listed as an unclean animal. The fangs like a vampire; a vampire sucks your blood from you.

Leviticus 17:11 New King James Version (NKJV)

[11] For the life of the flesh *is* in the blood

The unclean spirit came to suck the life out of me. Arthritis just does that it slowly sucks the life out of you over a period of time. The reason I accepted it was because the doctor told me that it was inherited from my mother who had it. It was a genetic curse that jumped on me. You may say why didn't you rebuke it in Jesus name? Glad you asked.

Remember I mentioned an act of unknown disobedience of an impression I should have listened to. Jan 26 1997 I had spent the night in Edmonton and was getting up early to get home to go back to work. I got up and looked outside to see that it raining a little bit. It wasn't raining hard and I thought I could make it home if I drove slowly because winter and rain are not a good combination. I had a strong impression to stay for a bit and go for lunch with my brother Richard. I thought that would be great but I need to get back to work in Grande Prairie. I got dressed and ready to leave when I had another impression. Just wait for a little bit and go on the computer on a chat line and visit with someone. Again I thought okay that would be great but I really have to get back because my boss was expecting me.

So I decided to go. After travelling a few blocks I did a brake test and realized it was very slippery. I decided if I travelled 10 kilometers an hour it would take three days to travel the three hundred miles back to Grande Prairie. After a few minutes the rain stopped and I did the brake test again and found I had traction. Quite pleased I picked up my speed as I noticed the sun coming out and drying the road. I continued through Edmonton, Spruce Grove, and stopped at Whitecourt for diner. Just outside of Whitecourt I realized it was slippery and slowed down only to get into a collision. This truck accident gave me a brain injury and post traumatic amnesia. It took me ten years to come out of that and in 2007 my mind suddenly cleared off and everything became normal again...

I mentioned that to show you how Satan took advantage of my injury and kick someone while he was down. Since then I have learned spiritual warfare even in dreams. I went to sleep one evening to be awakened by somebody crawling into bed with me. Must be dreaming, as I felt the individual pushing on me trying to push me out of bed. I pushed back trying to push it out of bed. We continued pushing each other not making progress, neither one of us. It seemed we were equally matched. I decided to use words and rebuke it because words are more powerful that human strength. I started to speak I command you in and suddenly its hand covered my mouth. I forcefully removed its hand from my mouth and said get out of my bed in Jesus name and gave it a shove with my foot and it fell out of my bed. I decided to stomp it with my foot since it was on the floor. I stomped the floor but it was gone. I sensed something behind me. I turned to see this 9-10 foot tall creature behind me. I turned and stood up and said I command you to get out of my house in Jesus name and you can leave through the basement window. I walked forward it backed up; I continued walking forward backing it up to the small basement window. It started to leave through the window and I said I command you to leave in Jesus name. The entity stopped and came back in and stood toe to toe with me. It had a smile on its face as it said "now you know I don't have to leave." I realized my mistake and said, "You have a choice, you can listen to me pray in tongues for three hours and worship the Holy Spirit or you can leave." When I said worship the Holy Spirit a disgusting look came over its face and it said Holy Spirit ugghhh. Then it just jumped through the window and out of my house. My mistake was I never believed my authority which became evident by having to tell the entity twice to leave. He sensed this and came back in. When I gave it the choice and ultimatum of worshipping the Holy Spirit it left because no matter how strong the devil likes to portray him, they want nothing to do with the awesome creator. Satan was totally defeated by Jesus at the cross and wants nothing to do with the creator anymore.

When Christians get the revelation of the authority Jesus gave them through the cross and shed blood they will walk in greater dimensions of spiritual authority. The next experience showed me this. Again I went to bed but my soul was a bit concerned so I went to sleep facing the direction the entity got into my bed. I thought if another one tried to get into bed it wouldn't get in from behind. Soul can get into silliness at times. If an entity wanted to get into my bed from behind it would just go to the other side. But for some reason I never thought of that. Again, a dream or maybe not. I was standing by my bed and I was surrounded by a python. The big snake was squeezing me. I struggled and struggled but felt it getting tighter. I rebuked it in Jesus name and I felt it begin to loosen on me. I struggled and finally got it from around me. I was holding it in my arms and pulling it off of me when I felt a pain in my back. It was intense like the snake had its teeth in my back and didn't want to let go. I said let me go in Jesus name and immediately it released me. As I held the snake it turned into a fluffy white cat purring gently in my arms. Its purring was trying to have a soothing effect on me. I thought no you don't I am not falling for that. A minute ago you were a snake holding me in bondage. I thought I am going to throw you outside. I proceeded up the stairs from my basement suite and opened the porch door to see two brown Rottweilers in the yard barking at me. I thought this should be fun throw the cat at the dogs and watch the dogs tear it apart. I threw the cat at the dogs and as soon as the cat landed it began to bark at the dogs. The dogs ignored the cat and continued to bark at me. I ignored the dogs went back in and woke up wondering about this experience.

The meaning of the dream is quite easy. The cat represented a familiar spirit that had kept me in bondage (the snake). A familiar spirit is a family spirit which brings curses from previous generation to the next. Rheumatoid arthritis has been a curse in my family for generations.

The idea is said to be based on certain statements in the Bible. For example:

Exodus 20:5 King James Version (KJV)

[5] Thou shalt not bow down thyself to them, nor serve them: for I the LORD thy God am a jealous God, visiting the iniquity of the fathers upon the children unto the third and fourth generation of them that hate me;

Exodus 34:6-7 King James Version (KJV)

[6] And the LORD passed by before him, and proclaimed, The LORD, The LORD God, merciful and gracious, longsuffering, and abundant in goodness and truth,

⁷ Keeping mercy for thousands, forgiving iniquity and transgression and sin, and that will by no means clear the guilty; visiting the iniquity of the fathers upon the children, and upon the children's children, unto the third and to the fourth generation.

Numbers 14:18King James Version (KJV)

¹⁸ The LORD is longsuffering, and of great mercy, forgiving iniquity and transgression, and by no means clearing the guilty, visiting the iniquity of the fathers upon the children unto the third and fourth generation.

Deuteronomy 5:9King James Version (KJV)

⁹ Thou shalt not bow down thyself unto them, nor serve them: for I the LORD thy God am a jealous God, visiting the iniquity of the fathers upon the children unto the third and fourth generation of them that hate me.

This is the curse of the law for walking in disobedience to God's word and laws. There is a big but in the equation, and that is, when we accept Jesus Christ as our saviour we are redeemed.

King James Bible Galatians 3:13
Christ hath redeemed us from the curse of the law, being made a curse for us: for it is written, Cursed *is* every one that hangeth on a tree:

2 Corinthians 5:21
God made Him who knew no sin to be sin on our behalf, so that in Him we might become the righteousness of God.

Here is the crux of the matter Satan through a familiar spirit attacked me with rheumatoid arthritis which has been in my family line for generations. At the time I was unaware of the benefits of the blood of Jesus even though I had been a Christian for decades. I accepted it not having the revelation that I was redeemed from it and the familiar spirit was attacking me illegally because I am no longer under the curse. The bible says in

Hosea 4:6 King James Bible
My people are destroyed for lack of knowledge: because thou hast rejected knowledge, I will also reject thee, that thou shalt be no priest to me: seeing thou hast forgotten the law of thy God, I will also forget thy children.

    The familiar spirit kept me in bondage because of my lack of knowledge. The Holy Spirit gave me this dream to help me understand why arthritis had gotten me. I repented on behalf of previous generations back to ten generations. I do not want this curse to continue to my children and future generations.

Romans 8:2

"For the law of the Spirit of life in Christ Jesus hath made me free from the law of sin and death."

The dogs represented mocking spirits and the cat barking at the dog and the dogs backing off from the cat showed authority structure in the kingdom of darkness. I believe I am now free from family curses and it won't continue on to my next generation. Thinking of the dogs, there may or may not be people who read this book and criticize it. Most people who critique and mock are full of misbeliefs or are of a dead religious nature. Carnal Christians can't handle supernatural events. Their minds just won't let them go there.

Romans 8:7 King James Version (KJV)

7 Because the carnal mind is enmity against God: for it is not subject to the law of God, neither indeed can be.

This next dream I would like to share is an instruction concerning other people. I attend a Thursday night bible study and we usually have many manifestations of the Holy Spirit. Two females stood out from the group that night and usually when someone stands out I usually write a psalm which is a prophetic poem for them. The meeting continued but all I had was a curiosity in me concerning these two individuals. I decided that I would pray about it at home that evening.

As I prayed I kept getting the impression that I was supposed to get oil and anoint them. I asked for a scripture because I won't do anything without the bible as my foundation. I kept thinking of when Samuel anointed David to be king and how he was the most unlikely of all his brothers. That actually fit these two because in the natural surely there is someone more charismatic, good looking, diplomatic and a people pleaser that would be a better candidate. I decided to ask God for a dream concerning the situation, simply because He talks to me quite frequently through dreams and visions. This dream began with me standing in front of an easel with a canvas on it. I had a paint brush in my hand. Jesus was standing beside me. The two girls were in front of us but one more to the right side and the other to the left side.

Jesus would look at one girl then turn to me and tell me what to paint. He then looked at the other girl and then tells me what to paint. Jesus continued looking at each girl a few times and in between each girl tells me what to paint. After a while a master portrait was painted. I mentioned to Jesus it was one portrait for both of them shouldn't it be one each. Jesus told me they have the same anointing but each will interpret the same portrait through different paradigms. I understood what He was saying; each woman was at different stages of growth and would interpret the portrait through the revelation of the Word of God that was in their individual lives. That was the confirmation I needed to anoint them the next bible study. I was instructed to use olive oil mixed with cinnamon powder to anoint Lori and Doris. Not necessarily their names but used for identity purpose rather than the two women, a little more closely to home.

That being settled my next thought was anoint them for what? I was to anoint them to flow as prophetic teachers. I could see that teaching ability in each of them but the prophetic part was stronger in one of them. Both had prophetic anointing just one walked deeper in it than the other.

    I am heavy on symbolism so I wondered why cinnamon mixed with olive oil. Cinnamon's figurative meaning from the Hebrew

The figurative meaning of cinnamon in the holy anointing oil can be taken from its Hebrew meaning "to erect or upright rolls." Also from its descriptive meaning *"sweet"* from the Hebrew being fragrant and spicy all rolled up into the spice of life that we find in living in the anointed life of the Lord Jesus Christ.

Olive oil can be a picture of the Holy Spirit, the One who sanctifies us, fills us, readies us to see Christ, and brings us light, joy, and spiritual health.

Olive oil can also be seen as a symbol of the Holy Spirit (or possibly of faith) in Jesus' Olive oil was sometimes used as a symbol of richness, joy, and health.

Wow the Lord has a great plan for Lori and Doris and I get to anoint them for it. I was thrilled. I kept thinking of the verse Jeremiah 29:11 New King James Version (NKJV)

[11] For I know the thoughts that I think toward you, says the LORD, thoughts of peace and not of evil, to give you a future and a hope.

As Doris and Lori move in the anointing which is teaching them they are going to be more like Jesus and people will see Jesus through their lives continually.

I went to the bible study the following Thursday and anointed them. I have watched them grow and develop a stronger more intimate with Jesus through the Holy Spirit as the years have gone by. I have had many dreams concerning different situations but I think you get the idea on how God can minister to you and through you this way. I want to take a look at visions in the next section.

VISIONS

What is a vision? The dictionary definition is

NOUN
1. the faculty or state of being able to see: "She had defective vision"
2. an experience of seeing someone or something in a dream or trance, or as a supernatural apparition: "The idea came to him in a vision"

VERB

Visions (third person present) ▢·▢ **visioned** (past tense) ▢·▢**visioned** (past participle) ▢·▢**visioning** (present participle)

The meaning of vision, means what God shows a particular person of what may happen in the future, it could be in dreams or it could well be in showing the future while he is awake.

What is biblical definition of vision?

In the Bible, visions are instruments of supernatural revelation. They are often means of communication, both visual and auditory, between Heavenly beings and people.

The meaning of Trance in the Bible (From *International Standard Bible Encyclopaedia*)

Trans (ekstasis): The condition expressed by this word is a mental state in which the person affected is partially or wholly unconscious of objective sensations, but intensely alive to subjective impressions which, however they may be originated, are felt as if they were revelations from without. They may take the form of visual or auditory sensations or else of impressions of taste, smell, heat or cold.

I gave you these two definitions to help you see that sometimes when in contact with heavenly beings you can experience an altered state of consciousness. In visions the Holy Spirit may reveal future things to you. When God reveals future things to you it is the revelation manifestation called the Word of Wisdom.

1 Corinthians 12:7 but the manifestation of the Spirit is given to every man to profit withal. ^{8}For to one is given by the Spirit the word of wisdom; to another the word of knowledge by the same Spirit.

The word of wisdom is a small piece of God's knowledge concerning future events.

Not the complete but a partial piece of the future. The word of knowledge is a piece of God's knowledge concerning past and or present events. Not the complete but partial again. Both are revelation gifts the body of Christ desperately need in these end times. I want to share a vision where I was in a trance like state. I knew where I was but when the vision started I was totally consumed by the vision. All reality ceased and the vision was the only thing I was aware of.

Instantly I went into a trance and a vision unfolded. Jesus was standing before me wearing the garments of a priest. We were standing beside a meadow with a creek running through it. Jesus bent down, picked a pebble from the creek and said, "You are like this pebble. I will clean you, shine you, and perfect you. Then I will place you back into this creek bed; this creek would not be complete without you." Then very emphatically the Lord said, 'I need you!'" The vision ended, I was totally thrilled at what I had seen.

You are part of the Body of Christ. God needs you, your church needs you, and I need you. Without you, the body is incomplete. I need you and you need me. Together we can function and see God's plans fulfilled in the earth.

The Holy Spirit through a trance gave me this vision to encourage me. Another vision that I have had repeatedly is; this one is not like a trance but more like looking in a window and watching it unfold. I find myself in the vision sitting in an open meadow up against a fruit tree. Jesus is sitting on the other side with his back against the tree same as I, in this vision I could hear very clear the words which were spoken, same as in the trance. Jesus said to me, "I will get you the bible college you think you need." I recognized a very patronizing tone in Jesus voice. I thought about this vision for a day or two then decided to go to Bible College. I did the third year and got my diploma in advanced teaching and pastoral studies. I received a lot of knowledge and was trained to think the way that denomination thought. Every denominational church thinks their organization is the right way. Everyone who is not like us needs to change because God has favor for my way of thinking thus saith me. By the time the year was up I was glad to go. I never attended graduation because my ride came four days early and I couldn't wait.

I am not against Bible College. If you believe God is calling you to go then by all means go, and go now. My spiritual father had taught us so well that Bible College was just an expensive refresher course. The Holy Spirit knew that when He gave me the vision. It wasn't more knowledge I needed but to develop a more intimate relationship with Him. The more intimate your relationship with the Holy Spirit then you receives wisdom to apply the knowledge you have. I have had a few conversations with Jesus under that fruit tree and it seems that I meet him there when something important needs discussing.

My next vision involves a young woman who couldn't have children. We will call this woman Ashleigh which may not be her real name, but just to make it more on a personal level. We were at a bible study in a little town in northwestern Alberta when this young woman came up for prayer. Apparently she had been to the doctors and found out she wasn't able to have children. She wanted prayer for this. As we prayed the Holy Spirit gave me a strong impression that I was to hold my bible flat in my hand and she was to strike it three times.

I held my bible flat and told her to strike it three times. She asked why and I said I don't know, just that I heard the Holy Spirit say to do it. She tapped the bible twice gently. Her grandma who is a godly woman said in a loud voice hit it hard. Ashleigh hit the bible hard the third time almost knocking it out of my hand. I was asked why and again I said I don't know but it is best to walk in obedience and trust God. We dismissed in prayer and after a little bit of fellowship I started the forty-five minute drive back to my home. About fifteen minutes from their house I had an open vision while driving.

An open vision is when you are completely aware of your surroundings and a vision like watching television appears in front of you. I was totally aware of the road and my ability to drive was still perfect. However in front of me appeared a vision of me what seemed like on a one hundred inch high definition television, with five point one surround sound. I was explaining to Ashleigh the natures of her three children. The first two would be just like her because she was a gentle shy and slightly timid girl. The third however would be a person of strong influence who would influence many for Jesus. Remember Ashleigh struck the bible gently twice but when yielded to the influence of a godly woman struck it hard the third time. She in the natural made a declaration through her actions to the spirit world.

Wow God was going to answer her prayer for children. I could hardly wait to go back to bible study next Thursday and share the vision with her. I shared the vision with the group and most kept silent. Ashleigh was sceptical to say the least. You could see in her eyes and countenance uncle you're crazy. We talked for a bit and she managed to stretch her faith and say maybe one but not three. During the week I had to visit her little town and chatted with her a couple of times about the vision. I noticed her thinking was starting to change as she would make playful jesting comments.

Next Thursday bible study was a turning point. Most people fail to realize that they set the course for their lives by the words they speak. Ashleigh made the declaration that she was only going to get pregnant twice. She stretched her faith to two children. That's great, people have to have faith and believe for themselves. How do you know what people believe? Listen to their words, that gives them away and most people if not all actually walk out in their lives the words that they continually speak.

A couple of weeks later Ashleigh told the bible study she had gotten pregnant. The group rejoiced and praised God with her. About a month or so Ashleigh went for an ultra sound and found out she was carrying twins. Life just continued on as normal and I would visit her once in a while encouraging her and even teasing her that maybe she might have a whole quiver of children. You could see in her stature that faith and belief were connecting. The evidence of the vision I had for her was coming to pass before her eyes. Many months had gone by and Thursday bible study was upon us again. Walking up to the house I met Ash on the sidewalk, she was talking to her aunt Lori. I had a strong impression of the number sixteen months. I mentioned this to Ash and Lori and they responded sixteen months in between the baby that's cool. Ashleigh gave birth to twin baby girls just like the vision said. The first two would be like her.

A few weeks later Ash text me and said she was pregnant. I responded with the words I heard in my spirit, "yes and he will be a boy and he is going to be a prophet before God." Needless to say after the ultra sound Ash confirmed it was a boy. She gave birth and fulfilled the vision of three children, two like her and the third one of strong influence. At the time of this writing the girls are eight and the boy is six. They are growing in Jesus with godly grandparents and relatives speaking into their lives. This godly mother stands before God in integrity and honor and raises her children to walk in the fear of the Lord as she does.

This next experience I want to share is unique. I put it in the category of visions simply because I am not sure. Was this a dream, a night vision, or an actual translation to heaven? I will share the experience and let you make your own judgment. I can so identify with what the apostle Paul was talking about in 2 Corinthians 12:21 King James Bible
I knew a man in Christ above fourteen years ago, (whether in the body, I cannot tell; or whether out of the body, I cannot tell: God knoweth ;) such a one caught up to the third heaven.

I put my head down on my pillow and closed my eyes and instantly I was in heaven. I was walking beside Jesus and noticed the expression on his face. It was an expression of solemn (not cheerful or smiling; serious) and concern mixed with sadness. We continued to walk until we came to a big iron door. We stopped at the door and I turned to Jesus and said, "You know what's in there." He said yes. I said, "It's the great white throne judgment." He said I know. I said, "Can I go in and watch?" He said; with a puzzled look on his face; "why do you want to watch that?" I said, "Because there is an aspect of our Father that no one knows and I want to know it." Jesus opened the door, let me in and closed the door behind me.

The room was dark and God the Father was clothed in a dark cloud. This room was a sad and foreboding place. Visually limited but emotionally enhanced. I believe that was because I was not allowed to see individual people but to feel the emotions of the event. I was there to see how this event affects God the Father not people. I was about to get a major revelation of the love of God for humanity. The emotions I felt were intensified more than I could ever imagine. The grief, sadness and utter hopelessness I experienced rocked my soul and entire being. The emotion I experienced was so intense that if it wasn't for the Holy Spirit protecting me I would be a crazy person in a mental ward today. The wild thing was it wasn't coming from the people being sentenced to the lake of fire. The emotion was coming from God the Father. After what seemed like an eternity I came out of the experience to find myself pacing in the front room. My bedroom is downstairs in the basement, how did I get upstairs to the living room? I don't know.

I was pacing and emotionally a wreck. I was crying out in anguish to the Holy Spirit, "You are the helper please help Father because He is hurting." I turned my focus to God the Father and asked, "Why are you in so much torment? What is wrong?" God the Father responded, "My creation whom I love with all my heart forced me to sentence them to a lake of fire. I had no choice because they took all choice away from me. That decision tears me up. They forced me by rejecting the plan of salvation through the shed blood of Jesus."

What a revelation God is a God of emotion not a hard nose individual sitting on a throne in heaven waiting for the chance to judge us? God is full of mercy and compassion and the affairs of mankind are before him always.

Psalm8:4 **New International Version**
what is mankind that you are mindful of them, human beings that you care for them?
New Living Translation
what are mere mortals that you should think about them, human beings that you should care for them?

English Standard Version
what is man that you are mindful of him, and the son of man that you care for him?

New American Standard Bible
What is man that you take thought of him, and the son of man that you care for him?

King James Bible
what is man, that thou art mindful of him? And the son of man, that thou visits him?

Holman Christian Standard Bible
what is man that you remember him, the son of man that you look after him?

International Standard Version
what is man that you take notice of him, or the son of man that you pay attention to him?

John 3:16 New International Version (NIV)

¹⁶ For God so loved the world that he gave his one and only Son, that whoever believes in him shall not perish but have eternal life.

Romans 10:8-13, **8** But what saith it? The word is nigh thee, *even* in thy mouth, and in thy heart: that is, the word of faith, which we preach; **9** that if thou shalt confess with thy mouth the Lord Jesus, and shalt believe in thine heart that God hath raised him from the dead, thou shalt be saved. **10** For with the heart man believeth unto righteousness; and with the mouth confession is made unto salvation. **11** For the scripture saith, whosoever believeth on him shall not be ashamed. **12** For there is no difference between the Jew and the Greek: for the same Lord over all is rich unto all that call upon him. **13** For whosoever shall call upon the name of the Lord shall be saved.

Pray Jesus come into my heart forgive me of all my sins. I believe that you died on the cross and paid for all my sins and that you raised from the dead. I believe you shed your blood for me to cleanse me of all sin and I receive you into my heart and declare with my mouth that you are Lord. According to your word I am saved and will spend eternity with you in heaven. Thank you Jesus: AMEN>

ENCOURAGEMENT

We are all on a journey through this life and pray that my journey will be a blessing to you. Many people struggle to get through life. And look for shortcuts. Please be careful. Satan will send you someone to help you find a shortcut.
Matthew 24:4 King James Bible
For many shall come in my name, saying, I am Christ; and shall deceive many.
The word Christ here is not Jesus last name, it means the anointed one. In this day and age we have many self-proclaimed prophets who make up things to get attention and money. People who are truly anointed will lead you to Jesus and focus on the Word of God.

BIO

William carries the anointing of a prophet and psalmist. He is also a Bible teacher, author and international speaker. He operates in all of the Spiritual gifts. He uses the gifts as the Holy Spirit wills. One of William's great desires is to lead others to Christ and to follow Holy Spirit wherever He leads.